Crime Prevention and Security Management

Series Editor
Martin Gill
Perpetuity Research
Tunbridge Wells, Kent, UK

It is widely recognized that we live in an increasingly unsafe society, but the study of security and crime prevention has lagged behind in its importance on the political agenda and has not matched the level of public concern. This exciting new series aims to address these issues looking at topics such as crime control, policing, security, theft, workplace violence and crime, fear of crime, civil disorder, white collar crime and anti-social behaviour. International in perspective, providing critically and theoretically-informed work, and edited by a leading scholar in the field, this series will advance new understandings of crime prevention and security management.

More information about this series at
http://www.palgrave.com/gp/series/14928

Colin King · Nicholas Lord

Negotiated Justice and Corporate Crime

The Legitimacy of Civil Recovery Orders and Deferred Prosecution Agreements

Colin King
School of Law
University of Sussex
Falmer, Brighton, UK

Nicholas Lord
School of Law
University of Manchester
Manchester, UK

Crime Prevention and Security Management
ISBN 978-3-319-78561-5   ISBN 978-3-319-78562-2 (eBook)
https://doi.org/10.1007/978-3-319-78562-2

Library of Congress Control Number: 2018936591

© The Editor(s) (if applicable) and The Author(s) 2018
This work is subject to copyright. All rights are solely and exclusively licensed by the Publisher, whether the whole or part of the material is concerned, specifically the rights of translation, reprinting, reuse of illustrations, recitation, broadcasting, reproduction on microfilms or in any other physical way, and transmission or information storage and retrieval, electronic adaptation, computer software, or by similar or dissimilar methodology now known or hereafter developed.
The use of general descriptive names, registered names, trademarks, service marks, etc. in this publication does not imply, even in the absence of a specific statement, that such names are exempt from the relevant protective laws and regulations and therefore free for general use.
The publisher, the authors and the editors are safe to assume that the advice and information in this book are believed to be true and accurate at the date of publication. Neither the publisher nor the authors or the editors give a warranty, express or implied, with respect to the material contained herein or for any errors or omissions that may have been made. The publisher remains neutral with regard to jurisdictional claims in published maps and institutional affiliations.

Cover illustration: © nemesis2207/Fotolia.co.uk

Printed on acid-free paper

This Palgrave Pivot imprint is published by the registered company Springer International Publishing AG part of Springer Nature
The registered company address is: Gewerbestrasse 11, 6330 Cham, Switzerland

Series Editor's Introduction

In this book, Colin King and Nicholas Lord (from the disciplines of law and criminology respectively) address one of the fundamental, yet largely unresolved issues of modern justice, namely how to hold criminal organisations to account. The context is one where the criminal justice process plays only a small part—and a very small one at that—in controlling their illegal behaviour and this is characterised by a distinct lack of appetite to prosecute.

Their scholarly accessible style will attract academics and practitioners to their work. Readers will engage with enlightening discussions on concepts of legitimacy and transparency (for example) as they relate to corporate crime. Running through their texts is a commitment to analysing how justice can be obtained, or rather how it is not currently achieved. They outline the limits of negotiated justice and discuss why incentivizing offending organisations to plead guilty is not an unqualified good. For example, in the case of self-reporting, they argue it 'has enabled corporates to negotiate their way *out* of the criminal process and the perception is that they are buying their way out of prosecution'.

They primarily focus their analysis via an examination of civil recovery orders (CROs) and deferred prosecution agreements (DPAs). They use case studies and are exhaustive in their coverage, indeed they analyse all eleven CROs and all four DPAs that have been used to date which predominantly relate to offences of bribery and/or corruption. They examine the advantages and disadvantages of each approach. This includes, for example, a focus on the limited practical alternatives on the one hand—not least given resource constraints—against the perception at least, and often the reality too on the other, that corporates are able to circumvent prosecution and pay to avoid justice by receiving a lesser penalty.

You will read about conflicts within the Asset Recovery Incentivisation Scheme (ARIS), and the different approaches to prosecution according to the perceptions of different leaders. And while the authors' central premise is that corporate crime *is* crime, and ought to be regarded as such, they concede that it rarely is. They point starkly to the inadequacy of corporate criminal liability laws in the UK and the limits of the doctrine of identification particularly for the big corporates which removes them from the gaze of punishment.

There are no magical solutions although the authors do outline what they feel will be the important factors to influence future developments. Most importantly perhaps, they remind us that it is vital for fairness that we hold wrongdoing to account and that in our search for alternatives to criminal prosecution, ones that work, we must not lose sight of a central point, that corporate crime is criminal and that the offender is a corporate rather than an individual does not make it any less so.

Tunbridge Wells, UK Martin Gill
February 2018

Acknowledgements

We would like to thank the many people with whom we have discussed these issues over the past few years, as well as those who have provided comments on earlier draft chapters. In alphabetical order, we thank Peter Alldridge; Liz Campbell; John Child; Jen Hendry; Saskia Hufnagel; Aleksandra Jordanoska; Mike Levi; Hannah Quirk; Clive Walker; and Dermot Walsh.

Thanks also to Josie Taylor and Steph Carey at Palgrave for their support in bringing this book to publication.

The funding of the Arts and Humanities Research Council (AHRC) Leadership Fellowship funding (Grant Ref: AH/P00640X/1) is gratefully acknowledged.

Contents

1 Negotiated Justice and Corporate Crime: An Introduction and Overview   1

2 Negotiated Justice and Enforcement Legitimacy   11

3 Civil Recovery Orders: Law, Policy and Practice   33

4 Deferred Prosecution Agreements: Law and Policy   67

5 Deferred Prosecution Agreements: In Practice   83

6 Calling to Answer?   117

Selected Bibliography   139

Index   149

About the Authors

Colin King is Reader in Law at the University of Sussex and co-Founder of the Crime Research Centre. He was an Academic Fellow at the Honourable Society of the Inner Temple from 2014–2017. In March 2016, Colin gave oral evidence at the Home Affairs Select Committee Inquiry into the Proceeds of Crime Act. Colin is co-editor of *The Handbook of Criminal and Terrorism Financing Law* (King, Walker, and Gurulé, Palgrave, 2018) and *Dirty Assets: Emerging Issues in the Regulation of Criminal and Terrorist Assets* (King and Walker, Ashgate, 2014). He is currently conducting empirical research on proceeds of crime legislation as part of an AHRC Leadership Fellowship.

Nicholas Lord is Reader in Criminology at the University of Manchester. His book *Regulating Corporate Bribery in International Business* (2014, Ashgate) was the winner of the British Society of Criminology Book Prize 2015 and he was the winner of the Young Career Award 2014 of the American Society of Criminology's Division of White-Collar Crime. He has a forthcoming co-edited book on *Corruption in Commercial Criminal Enterprise* (Campbell and Lord, Routledge, 2018). Nicholas is currently undertaking research funded by the PaCCS; British Academy; Alcohol Research UK; N8; and White & Case LLP. He is also the President of the European Working Group on Organisational and White-Collar Crime (EUROC) hosted within the European Society of Criminology.

LIST OF TABLES

Table 2.1	Civil recovery orders obtained by the SFO and CRU	17
Table 2.2	Deferred prosecution agreements obtained by the SFO	21
Table 4.1	Purported advantages and disadvantages of DPAs	75
Table 5.1	Overall calculation (Rolls Royce DPA)	105

CHAPTER 1

Negotiated Justice and Corporate Crime: An Introduction and Overview

Abstract This chapter provides an overview of the book and the contention that 'accommodation' of corporate crime—rather than criminal prosecution—is increasingly the 'new normal'.

Keywords Corporate crime · Enforcement · Criminal law · Accommodation

CONTEXT

Imagine: a drug dealer—someone like Walter White from the series *Breaking Bad*—walks into a police station and says: '*I want to confess. I am a drug dealer. I am sorry for my actions, and want to put things right.*' If Walter also provides detailed evidence of the millions of dollars that he has made from his illegal activities, and assuming that there are no issues relating to the admissibility of his confession, for example, it might be expected that Walter would be prosecuted and likely convicted. There might be some leniency shown at the sentencing stage given his cooperation, but even so the likelihood is that Walter would be sentenced to prison. Or, what of a student who, having received a fail mark on a dissertation, attempts to bribe his professor to pass him? That is what 26 year old Yang Li did having received a mark of 37% for his Masters dissertation. After the attempted bribe was rebuffed, and as

© The Author(s) 2018
C. King and N. Lord, *Negotiated Justice and Corporate Crime*, Crime Prevention and Security Management,
https://doi.org/10.1007/978-3-319-78562-2_1

1

the student was putting the money back in his bag, a replica handgun loaded with six pellets fell to the floor. Yang Li admitted charges of bribery and possessing an imitation firearm. He was sentenced to 12 months in prison for bribery and 6 months on the firearm charge (to run concurrently) and was also ordered to pay prosecution costs.[1] What, though, of corporate wrongdoing: what should happen to a corporate that engages in criminal conduct? If the Managing Director or the Chief Executive Officer of a corporate (or, more likely, a solicitor on behalf of that corporate) were to self-report to the authorities that that corporate had engaged in 'questionable conduct', it would be no surprise were a 'civil settlement'[2] agreed between that corporate and the authorities. Indeed, our argument in this book is that such 'accommodation' of corporate wrongdoing—rather than criminal prosecution—is increasingly the 'new normal'.[3]

Our focus in this book is to explore how wrongdoing on the part of corporates is being 'differentially enforced'.[4] This was a theme central to the seminal work of Edwin Sutherland on white-collar crime; Sutherland argued that those persons of the upper socioeconomic class, in particular business and corporate elites, engage in much criminal behaviour but that these crimes differ principally in the administrative procedures which are used to deal with them (i.e. non-criminal responses).[5] For this reason, a strong sense of injustice underpinned his analysis, as the poor were pursued through criminal justice while the affluent, respectable

---

[1] See Press Association, 'Failing Student Jailed for Trying to Bribe Professor', *The Guardian* (April 23, 2013).

[2] Note that the word 'settlement' is often used by enforcement agencies in this context: see, for example, SFO Press Release, 'Oxford Publishing Ltd to Pay Almost £1.9 Million as Settlement After Admitting Unlawful Conduct in Its East African Operations' (July 3, 2012).

[3] Contrary to discourse emanating from the Serious Fraud Office. See, for example, Graham Ruddick, 'Serious Fraud Office Boss Warns Big Names to Play Ball—or Else', *The Observer* (April 2, 2017).

[4] Celia Wells, 'Containing Corporate Crime. Civil or Criminal Controls?', in James Gobert and Ana-Maria Pascal (eds), *European Developments in Corporate Criminal Liability* (Routledge, 2011), p. 16.

[5] Edwin H. Sutherland, *White Collar Crime: The Uncut Version* (Yale University Press, 1983), p. 7.

businessperson exploited their privileged positions and power to evade the criminal courts.[6] Using the lens of negotiated justice and legitimacy, we examine these enforcement dynamics in the UK in relation to corporate financial crime. More specifically, we scrutinise how civil recovery orders (CROs) under the Proceeds of Crime Act 2002 and deferred prosecution agreements (DPAs) under the Crime and Courts Act 2013 are used in response to corporate wrongdoing.[7] Given that there is criminal activity involved, we explore the preference for 'settlement' rather than criminal prosecution.

Genesis of the Book

We (the authors of this book) both worked in the same university from 2013 to 2015. During that time (and afterwards) we had a number of conversations on corporate crime, (the lack of) criminal prosecutions, the preference for civil settlements, and proposals for (and ultimately legislation providing for) DPAs. We were intrigued by the preference for negotiation with (and accommodation of) corporates, rather than prosecution. We deliberated how, and why, corporates manage to avoid actual prosecution for what is clearly criminal conduct, and the lack of transparency surrounding deals done behind closed doors. For a long time, we discussed potential collaboration—drawing upon our backgrounds in law and criminology, and particularly our research interests in corporate crime[8] and proceeds of crime.[9] When the first DPA was announced in November 2015, we resolved to finally put our thoughts down on paper. After collaborating on a book chapter examining 'negotiated

---

[6] James Gobert and Maurice Punch, *Rethinking Corporate Crime* (Butterworths, 2003), p. 4. See also David O. Friedrichs, *Trusted Criminals: White Collar Crime in Contemporary Society* (4th ed, Wadsworth, 2009).

[7] We deliberately do not engage with CROs against individuals nor with criminal prosecution of officials from corporates (see, for example, prosecutions of former senior employees of the F.H. Bertling group: SFO Press Release, 'Three Men Sentenced in $20m Angolan Oil Corruption Case' (October 20, 2017)). It is also worth noting that DPAs can only be agreed with corporates, they are not available to individuals.

[8] E.g. Nicholas Lord, *Regulating Corporate Bribery in International Business: Anti-corruption in the UK and Germany* (Ashgate, 2014).

[9] E.g. Colin King, 'Using Civil Processes in Pursuit of Criminal Law Objectives: A Case Study of Non-Conviction Based Asset Forfeiture', *International Journal of Evidence and Proof* (2012), 16(4): 337.

non-contention' in the context of transnational corporate bribery,[10] we decided to expand our focus—the result being this book.

This book explores a significant, contemporary issue that is fast evolving, namely the use of CROs and DPAs as a response to corporate crime. Indeed, it is certainly timely as we approach the final few months of David Green's reign as Director of the Serious Fraud Office (SFO).[11] Corporate crime, and the enforcement response thereto, has attracted significant attention in the UK in recent years. For example, the SFO was established following the 'Roskill Report'[12] to act as an investigator *and* prosecutor of serious and complex frauds.[13] Prior to the establishment of the SFO, successive UK governments had displayed a lack of interest in commercial/corporate crime. In recent years, however, the SFO's continued existence has come under threat following critique relating to a lack of prosecutions,[14] collapsed cases,[15] failed investigations,[16] and data loss.[17] Despite facing threats of being abolished, or subsumed into other agencies, the SFO continues as the main enforcement agency in the area of corporate financial crime—with its position arguably strengthened following significant settlements with Rolls Royce[18]

---

[10] Nicholas Lord and Colin King, 'Negotiating Non-Contention: Civil Recovery and Deferred Prosecution in Response to Transnational Corporate Bribery', in Liz Campbell and Nicholas Lord (eds), *Corruption in Commercial Enterprise: Law, Theory and Practice* (Routledge, 2018).

[11] This book was submitted for publication in January 2018. By the time of publication, David Green will have stepped down as Director. See Lucy Burton and Christopher Williams, 'SFO boss David Green kicks-start talks with legal giants as successors circle', *The Telegraph* (November 4, 2017).

[12] Lord Roskill (Chair), *Fraud Trials Committee Report* (HM Stationery Office, 1986); Michael Levi, 'Fraud in the Courts: Roskill in Context', *British Journal of Criminology* (1986), 26(4): 394.

[13] Criminal Justice Act 1987, Part 1.

[14] John Moylan, 'Serious Fraud Office: A Chequered History', *BBC News* (August 22, 2012).

[15] Tom Harper, 'Victor Dahdaleh Corruption Case: Billionaire's Fraud Trial Collapses After Key SFO Witnesses Refuse to Give Evidence', *The Independent* (December 10, 2013).

[16] Simon Bowers, 'SFO Abandons Corruption Inquiry into Tchenguiz and Kaupthing', *The Guardian* (October 15, 2012).

[17] Rob Evans, 'Serious Fraud Office Admits Losing Thousands of Documents Linked to BAE', *The Guardian* (August 8, 2013).

[18] Nils Pratley, 'Rolls-Royce's SFO Settlement Is Big, Ugly and Serious', *The Guardian* (January 16, 2017).

and Tesco plc.[19] Yet, even such settlements did not stop criticism and threats of being abolished.[20] Such plans have been put on hold for the moment however, following the 2017 General Election result (when the Conservative Party failed to secure an overall majority). Shortly after the election, the SFO announced its decision to prosecute Barclays (and former directors), which was said to have granted the SFO a reprieve[21] and, in September 2017, the start of the process to recruit a new SFO Director seemingly confirmed that the SFO is here to stay (at least for the time being).[22] There have been suggestions that with the enactment of DPAs, the SFO's bark is no longer mightier than its bite; indeed, it might be that the availability of DPAs might well provide a new impetus for the SFO in tackling corporate crime.

When David Green took over as Director in April 2012, he was keen to reinforce the SFO's purpose as a 'key crime fighting agency targeting top-end fraud, bribery and corruption.[23] As he stated later that summer: 'Let me make this clear. In any case where there is a realistic prospect of conviction and it is in the public interest to prosecute then SFO will prosecute, whether the defendant is an individual or a corporate'.[24] In September 2012 he further outlined his envisioned SFO purpose:

> As to the SFO's approach. Generally, if we have sufficient evidence and it is in the public interest to prosecute, we will do so. At the same time, I am very much in favour of maximising the tools available to us as investigators and prosecutors.
>
> Most topical among those tools are Deferred Prosecution Agreements. These would provide, in the right circumstances and under judicial supervision, a way of addressing usually historic and self-reported corporate misconduct justly without the collateral damage of a criminal conviction.

---

[19] Graham Ruddick and Julia Kollewe, 'Tesco to Pay £129m Fine Over Accounting Scandal', *The Independent* (March 28, 2017).

[20] Caroline Binham and Jane Croft, 'Tories Pledge to Abolish Serious Fraud Office—Manifesto', *Financial Times* (May 18, 2017).

[21] Alan Tovey and Ben Martin, 'SFO Granted a Reprieve from Plans to Scrap It a Day After Barclays Charges', *The Telegraph* (June 21, 2017).

[22] Christopher Williams, 'Theresa May Abandons Plans to Scrap Fraud Office', *The Telegraph* (September 16, 2017).

[23] SFO Press Release, 'New SFO Director David Green' (April 23, 2012).

[24] SFO Press Release, '10th Annual Corporate Accountability Conference' (June 14, 2012).

> Of course, we need to articulate why companies should self report (what is in it for them) and they need to be encouraged to do so. ...
> Civil settlements will continue to be offered and reached in appropriate cases. ... Responding to recent OECD recommendations, we were careful to explain publicly why such a settlement [*i.e. with Oxford Publishing Ltd*] was the appropriate course in the particular circumstances of that case, namely the impossibility of obtaining evidence.[25]

It is these strategies that we scrutinise in this book: since Green took over at the SFO, his prosecutorial rhetoric has continued, but within a context whereby most cases of corporate financial crime have been concluded through non-prosecution based strategies, using tools such as CROs and DPAs. We see that the focus in England and Wales increasingly appears to be on DPAs. In contrast, DPAs are not available to Scottish authorities, and it appears that they are willing to use CROs, particularly in cases of transnational bribery.

In exploring such enforcement approaches, we were keen to contribute to the academic and practitioner literature as it is developing. Indeed, as we write, it is rumoured that a fifth DPA is under negotiation between the SFO and a corporate—rumoured to be Airbus.[26] It is also expected that a number of current investigations (such as that relating to Unaoil[27]) might end up being resolved through DPAs.[28] For these reasons, we were attracted to the Palgrave Pivot series with the quick publication process.[29]

---

[25] SFO Press Release, 'Cambridge Symposium 2012' (September 3, 2012).

[26] Nick Kochan, 'Airbus in Talks to Settle Fraud Claims for £1 Billion', *Evening Standard* (September 15, 2017). Others, however, suggest that the SFO investigation could take years: see 'Airbus Faces Lengthy Probe, No Quick Fine: Sources', *Reuters* (September 15, 2017).

[27] See SFO Press Release, 'Unaoil Investigation' (July 19, 2016).

[28] It is noticeable, though, that the investigation into Barclays will not result in a DPA: see SFO Press Release, 'SFO Charges in Barclays Qatar Capital Raising Case' (June 20, 2017); Caroline Binham, 'Position Taken by Barclays Ruled Out DPA Deal with Fraud Agency', *Financial Times* (June 22, 2017).

[29] A traditional law or criminology article would not allow us to go into the depth that we want. Moreover, the inherent delay from writing to publication of a journal article was an important consideration. Furthermore, rather than spend two years or so on a monograph of approximately 100,000+ words, we wanted to feed into the literature as it is developing.

KEY THESIS AND OUTLINE OF BOOK

In our view, there is a strong normative argument for using the criminal law as a primary response to corporate crime. In practice, we see that corporate crimes are not always (indeed rarely) dealt with by criminal prosecution, whether for practical and pragmatic reasons (e.g. evidential difficulties), or ideological and normative reasons (e.g. preferences to attempt to persuade corporates to comply, or protect national economic interests).[30] It is under these conditions that we see authorities reverting to the use of CROs and DPAs. However, difficulties in enforcement ought not be an excuse for sidestepping criminal law responses; if there are difficulties with the application of the criminal law, then that is an issue that should be re-visited.[31] We recognise, however, the reality that CROs and DPAs are being used; where this does happen, the decisions behind such diversion need to be transparently and openly articulated, justified and explained to regulated communities and the public more widely. While these mechanisms may be desirable for, or reflect the interests of, particular groups, such as large corporates, they may not correspond with the public interest where social equality, fairness and justice is expected. Indeed, there may even exist a perception that corporate wrongdoers are able to negotiate, or buy, their way out of prosecution.[32] To examine these dynamics, our book is structured as follows.

In Chapter 2 we locate the regulation and enforcement of corporate crimes within the conceptual frameworks of 'negotiated justice' and 'legitimacy'. There is an extensive literature on negotiated justice, its meaning and nature, but one that is predominantly concerned with the inducement of guilty pleas for 'volume' crimes through incentivisation. In the chapter we present a framework for understanding the legitimacy of enforcement responses to corporate financial crimes that are underpinned by processes of negotiation as seen in the use of CROs and DPAs. For instance, states criminalise behaviours in part because they are recognised to be inherently 'bad'; there is a strong moral (and political)

---

[30] These issues are discussed further in Chapter 6.

[31] See, for example, Ministry of Justice, *Corporate Liability for Economic Crime, Call for Evidence* (Cm 9370) (January 2017).

[32] See Nicola Padfield, 'Deferred Prosecution Agreements', *Archbold Review* (2012), 7: 4.

dimension to criminalisation. But how can justice be negotiated when there is no admission of guilt from implicated corporations? What are the implications for social fairness and moral/procedural equality if state authorities negotiate non-criminal sanctions with corporations for harmful, criminal behaviours in the absence of a guilty admission? How do we establish whether negotiated justice is a legitimate state response? This chapter lays the foundations of these questions. In the chapter we provide an overview of all cases that have used CROs and DPAs to date. Of these, all eleven CROs and three (of the four) DPAs are concerned with offences of bribery and/or corruption. Consequently, much of our discussion relates to those offences (rather than corporate crime more generally, though the arguments are equally applicable to other areas of corporate wrongdoing).

Chapter 3 explores the development of civil recovery as an enforcement tool in the context of corporate crime. CROs were first used by the SFO in 2008 and by the Scottish Civil Recovery Unit in 2012. Specifically, we explore the preference for 'civil settlement', with the consequence that corporate wrongdoers can avoid criminal prosecution. The emphasis on settlement, however, does give rise to a number of concerns, which we explore. For example, one criticism is that civil settlements (the term is deliberately used here, given its use by the SFO and others) enable corporates to avoid prosecution, with the perception that they can 'buy' their way out of trouble. Another criticism has been the lack of transparency in the negotiation process. It was only following significant criticism that a shift towards more openness became apparent, though not all problems have been addressed. A further issue to be considered in this chapter is the different approach adopted in Scotland, namely that as the rest of the UK moves away from CROs, such powers remain an important cog in the Scottish enforcement response to corporate crime.

In Chapters 4 and 5 we analyse DPAs. Chapter 4 examines the law and policy relating to their implementation. The DPA regime was introduced in 2014 and provided the SFO with a criminal law sanctioning possibility for corporations involved in a wide range of serious financial crimes. DPAs enable the SFO to circumvent the pragmatic obstacles to the criminal prosecution of corporations (e.g. the restrictions of the 'identification' principle) but also represent ideological and normative preferences of state actors for negotiating justice in cases of serious corporate financial crimes. In the chapter we identify advantages and disadvantages with the regime, making cross-jurisdictional comparisons with the US where appropriate. Chapter 5 then explores how DPAs have been used in practice. To do this, we analyse all four cases where DPAs have been negotiated to provide concrete insights into how law and policy translates into practice, and identify key issues with the approach. Furthermore, we conceptualise the processes inherent in agreeing deferred prosecution (i.e. negotiation, cooperation, reformation) and the associated outcomes, questioning whether 'justice' can really be achieved through DPAs and, if so, what this should look like, or whether DPAs represent an extended 'accommodation' of corporate crimes by the state.

In the final chapter we reinforce our argument that corporate crime *is* crime and ought to be dealt with as such. This statement might appear relatively straightforward, but the reality of responding to corporate crime is anything but straightforward. Considering the enforcement focus on non/deferred prosecution options—particularly CROs and DPAs, as discussed in Chapters 3–5—the reality is that corporate crime is rarely prosecuted in the criminal courts (albeit with some exceptions). Part of the problem here is the inadequacy of corporate criminal liability laws in the UK, though there are other reasons including executive interference to prevent criminal prosecution (e.g. BAE Systems). In this chapter, we argue in favour of a criminal law-focused approach to corporate wrongdoing. Such an approach serves an important communicative function—calling wrongdoers to account, as well as expressing societal condemnation of the activity in question. Further, in this chapter we engage with debates about the value of criminal action—given that any punishment will be monetary, regardless of whether proceedings are criminal or otherwise.

In sum, our core thesis in this book is that for *criminal justice* to be accomplished, and for associated enforcement to be seen as legitimate, just and fair, corporate crime ought to be dealt with through corresponding criminal law sanctioning mechanisms. In reality, we often see the social and political downgrading of these behaviours, through state decisions instead to pursue *regulatory* and/or *civil* justice underpinned by negotiation, rather then contention. Preferences for regulatory and/or civil justice, while pragmatic, do not always represent justice in cases of corporate crime. We see this as a means of *accommodating* corporate crime. Of course, there are multifarious economic pressures (e.g. availability of resources), and/or normative and ideological preferences of the executive, that explain why strategies of non-prosecution and non-criminal sanctioning are pursued. But where fractures appear between the rule of law in theory and practice, where the performance of the enforcement authorities deviates away from expected values of justice and social fairness, and where regulated communities are sceptical to engage with these strategies, we see a deficit in legitimacy emerge.

CHAPTER 2

Negotiated Justice and Enforcement Legitimacy

Abstract This chapter situates our discussion within the conceptual frameworks of 'negotiated justice' and 'legitimacy'. This chapter sets out the framework for understanding the legitimacy of enforcement responses to corporate crime, laying the groundwork for discussion of Civil Recovery Orders (CROs) and Deferred Prosecution Agreements (DPAs) in subsequent chapters. This chapter provides an overview of all cases that have used CROs and DPAs to date.

Keywords Corporate crime · Negotiated justice · Guilty plea · Social fairness · Legitimacy · Serious Fraud Office

INTRODUCTION

In this chapter we locate the regulation and enforcement of corporate financial crimes within the conceptual framework of 'negotiated justice'. There is an extensive literature on negotiated justice, its meaning and nature, but one that is predominantly concerned with the inducement of (guilty) pleas for 'volume' crimes through incentivisation. The negotiation of justice is a phenomenon that requires analysis from both legal and social scientific perspectives to allow us to understand both the rules and practices that guide what negotiation looks like and the inherent processes involved in how it is carried out. In this book we integrate our legal and social scientific/criminological knowledge to better understand

© The Author(s) 2018
C. King and N. Lord, *Negotiated Justice and Corporate Crime*, Crime Prevention and Security Management,
https://doi.org/10.1007/978-3-319-78562-2_2

how justice is being negotiated by corporations implicated in criminal behaviours of a financial nature. From the perspective of prosecutors, the benefits include the certainty of a 'success' (whether of a criminal conviction, a civil settlement, or otherwise). For example, where a defendant agrees to plead guilty (even if to a lesser charge than originally envisaged), the prosecution do not run the risk of an acquittal at trial. At a time of strained resources and budgetary austerity, the appeal to prosecutors is obvious, not least that it allows efficient disposal of a case and frees up time/resources to work on other cases. These points are evident in the context of civil recovery orders (CROs) and deferred prosecution agreements (DPAs) as responses to corporate crime.

The concept of 'negotiated justice' is not new. In the US context, Donald Cressey recognised that a process occurs within the legal apparatus for dealing with delinquents and criminals whereby some are selected for 'counting' within official statistics and others are ignored. This process makes some social problems (i.e. crime) an artefact of the methodologies used to generate statistical facts about them—the processes inherent in the criminal justice system are therefore central to understanding the nature of the crime phenomenon:

> [R]ecent studies of police and court operations are beginning to indicate that the crime a person is said to have committed, and even the decisions about whether he is a criminal or not, depend upon the outcome of negotiations he conducts with criminal justice administrators.[1]

For Cressey, this procedural phenomenon represented a contradiction in terms—'negotiated justice'—given the extent to which both law enforcement authorities and many criminal courts at that time were organised in a way that ensured most cases would be disposed of without trial. He further argued that judges perceived the extended negotiation of justice in this way as both necessary and a problem in need of solving. This problem was in part practical as there were insufficient numbers within the legal system to manage if all cases went to trial. As Cressey indicates, a key conclusion by various appellate courts, the President's Commission and the American Bar Association was that processes of negotiation and related plea-bargaining ought to be regularised and formalised by being made legitimate, open and more visible. However, a fundamental question remained for Cressey 'as to

---

[1] Donald R. Cressey, 'Negotiated Justice', *Criminology* (1968), 5(4): 5.

whether justice that is negotiated is commensurate with fundamental democratic legal principles, whether the negotiations are carried out in public or not'.[2] We explore such questions in this book.

NEGOTIATED JUSTICE AND CORPORATE CRIMES

Negotiating justice and plea-bargaining are now central and formal features of the criminal justice system in the US.[3] Similarly 'the centrality of the plea' is evident in the UK,[4] with a wide array of incentives for an early guilty plea.[5] There are many reasons why a person might plead guilty, for example the hope of a lighter sentence or charge reduction.[6] While it might be thought that a person would only plead guilty if s/he were in fact guilty, there is also evidence of pressure to plead guilty contrary to the original intention to contest the charge.[7] Concern has also been expressed in relation to 'the increasing pressure for administrative "justice" and the continued erosion of due process rights'.[8]

Much of the (UK) literature on 'negotiated justice' has tended to focus on 'ordinary' and conventional forms of crimes, rather than on serious

---

[2] Donald R. Cressey, 'Negotiated Justice', *Criminology* (1968), 5(4): 9.

[3] See Richard L. Lippke, *The Ethics of Plea Bargaining* (Oxford University Press, 2011). For discussion of its origins, see Mary E. Vogel, 'The Social Origins of Plea Bargaining: Conflict and the Law in the Process of State Formation, 1830–1860', *Law and Society Review* (1999), 33(1): 161. See also Mary E. Vogel, *Coercion to Compromise: Plea Bargaining, the Courts, and the Making of Political Authority* (Oxford University Press, 2007).

[4] Penny Darbyshire, 'The Mischief of Plea Bargaining and Sentencing Rewards', *Criminal Law Review* (2000), 895, 896. See also JUSTICE, *Negotiated Justice: A Closer Look at the Implications of Plea Bargains* (JUSTICE, 1993); Aogán Mulcahy, 'The Justification of Justice—Legal Practitioners' Accounts of Negotiated Case Settlements in Magistrates' Courts', *British Journal of Criminology* (1994), 34: 411.

[5] See, for example, Criminal Justice Act 2003, s.144 'Reduction in Sentences for Guilty Pleas'; Sentencing Council, *Reduction in Sentence for a Guilty Plea: Definitive Guideline* (March 2017).

[6] David Moxon and Carol Hedderman, 'Mode of Trial Decisions and Sentencing Differences Between Courts', *Howard Journal of Criminal Justice* (1994), 33(2): 97.

[7] John Baldwin and Michael McConville, *Negotiated Justice: Pressures to Plead Guilty* (Martin Robertson and Co Ltd, 1977). For further discussion of legal and extra-legal pressures, see Kevin Kwok-yin Cheng, 'Pressures to Plead Guilty: Factors Affecting Plea Decisions in Hong Kong's Magistrates' Courts', *British Journal of Criminology* (2013), 53: 257.

[8] Ralph Henham, 'Further Evidence on the Significance of Plea in the Crown Court', *Howard Journal of Criminal Justice* (2002), 41(2): 151.

corporate crimes of a financial nature[9] (albeit with some exceptions[10]). In the context of corporate wrongdoing, the concern is not so much on due process rights *in* the criminal process; rather the concern is whether corporates are negotiating their way *out* of the criminal process. That is the focus of our analysis in this book. While the corporate crime literature has engaged with debates over whether negotiation and persuasion, or more punitive responses, are most 'effective' in changing corporate behaviour and achieving 'justice', in practice we see admixtures of these approaches to enable more responsive interactions.[11] With this in mind, this book specifically explores how applicable the concept of 'negotiated justice' is to corporate crimes, with specific consideration of the legitimacy of this approach. More specifically, we are concerned with the legitimacy of CROs and DPAs, which will be discussed in the next three chapters.

While there are often comparisons between settlements in response to corporate wrongdoing (whether DPAs, CROs, or otherwise) and plea bargaining, it is important to emphasise that with plea bargains the defendant usually pleads guilty to an offence. That is not the case with either DPAs or CROs. Hence, it is useful to also cast an eye towards another aspect of the criminal justice system where 'negotiation' can come into play, namely diversion (or those decisions that determine whether a case is dealt with as 'criminal'). Indeed, the origins of US DPAs can be traced to pre-trial diversion approaches for juvenile offenders (though it must be acknowledged that 'the application of these prosecution tools has been reversed, since they were initially intended for minor crime cases, whereas nowadays they can be stipulated even for

---

[9] It is notable that the Attorney General did publish Guidelines on Plea Discussions in Cases of Serious or Complex Fraud in 2009. For further discussion, see Daniele Alge, 'Negotiated Plea Agreements in Cases of Serious and Complex Fraud in England and Wales: A New Conceptualisation of Plea Bargaining?', *European Journal of Current Legal Issues* (2013), 19(1).

[10] In the white-collar and corporate crime literature, the centrality of negotiation (and associated concerns) in the response to corporate crime is a common theme: e.g. Hazel Croall, 'Combating Financial Crime: Regulatory Versus Crime Control Approaches', *Journal of Financial Crime* (2000), 11(1): 45; Celia Wells, 'Corporate Crime: Opening the Eyes of the Sentry', *Legal Studies* (2010), 30(3): 370.

[11] See Nicholas Lord, *Regulating Corporate Bribery in International Business: Anti-corruption in the UK and Germany* (Ashgate, 2014); Michael Levi and Nicholas Lord, 'White-Collar and Corporate Crimes', in Alison Liebling, Shadd Maruna, and Lesley McAra (eds), *The Oxford Handbook of Criminology* (6th ed, Oxford University Press, 2017) for an overview of the regulatory literature relating to white-collar and corporate crimes.

high-profile cases involving companies "too big to jail"').[12] As Ashworth and Redmayne note, 'The attractions of diversion are that it aims to be simpler, cheaper, less bureaucratic (cutting police paperwork); it is a more proportionate and less stigmatic response to many minor offences; and it appears to be no less effective, in terms of reconvictions, than conviction and sentence'.[13]

To take one example: the conditional caution can be given to a person[14] aged 18 or over once certain requirements are met. These requirements are set out in section 23 of the Criminal Justice Act 2003:

1. The authorised person must have evidence that the person has committed an offence;
2. A relevant prosecutor determines that there is sufficient evidence to charge the person with the offence[15] and that a conditional caution should be given in respect of the offence;
3. The person must admit that s/he committed the offence in question;
4. The authorised person must explain the effect of the conditional caution to the person and warn him/her that failure to comply with any of the specified conditions may result in him/her being prosecuted for the offence;
5. The person must sign a document containing: details of the offence, an admission that s/he committed the offence, consent to being given the conditional caution, and the conditions that attach to that caution.

The conditions that may attach to a conditional caution can be aimed at facilitating the rehabilitation of the person, ensuring that she makes

[12] Federico Mazzacuva, 'Justifications and Purposes of Negotiated Justice for Corporate Offenders: Deferred and Non-prosecution Agreements in the UK and US Systems of Criminal Justice', *Journal of Criminal Law* (2014), 249, 255.

[13] Andrew Ashworth and Mike Redmayne, *The Criminal Process* (5th ed, Oxford University Press, 2010), p. 164. Bronitt submits that DPAs ought to be regarded as 'diversionary tools of preventive justice'. Simon Bronitt, 'Regulatory Bargaining in the Shadows of Preventive Justice: Deferred Prosecution Agreements', in Tamara Tulich, Rebecca Ananian-Welsh, Simon Bronitt, and Sarah Murray (eds), *Regulating Preventive Justice: Principle, Policy and Paradox* (Routledge, 2017).

[14] Described as 'the offender'.

[15] The Full Code Test in the Code for Crown Prosecutors must be satisfied here. See CPS, The Full Code Test, available at: https://www.cps.gov.uk/publication/full-code-test (last accessed January 11, 2018). See also Ministry of Justice, *Code of Practice for Adult Conditional Cautions: Part 3 of the Criminal Justice Act 2003* (January 2013), para. 2.2.

reparation for the offence, and/or punishing her.[16] Conditions must be appropriate, proportionate, and achievable.[17] When a conditional caution is given, criminal proceedings for the offence in question are halted and the person is given the opportunity to comply with specified conditions. If the person fails, without reasonable excuse, to comply with the specified conditions then criminal proceedings can be instituted for the offence in question and the conditional caution will cease to have effect.[18] It is important to stress, though, that the decision whether or not to give a conditional caution will include consideration of the *seriousness* of the offence.[19] Indeed: 'An assessment of the seriousness of the offence is the starting point for considering whether a Conditional Caution may be appropriate. The more serious the offence, the less likely a Conditional Caution will be appropriate'.[20]

While there may be arguments in favour of diversion in relation to low-level crime, it might be suggested that serious crime—such as bribery and corruption—ought more appropriately be dealt with by the criminal law. Indeed, contrary to the process adopted with diversion, with some corporate crimes we see justice negotiated where admissions of guilt are not even required, as in cases where CROs and/or DPAs are used. This is an important distinction and is the starting point of our analysis of CROs and DPAs, and their legitimacy as enforcement responses. Within these complex scenarios, we see legitimacy as a linear, not a binary, concept, with varying shades of 'legitimate', and we recognise that it is the mixture of these various factors that dictate whether different state responses, such as those that inhere negotiated justice, are more, or less, legitimate.

At this point, it is useful to set out details of all CROs and DPAs that are concerned with corporate wrongdoing. Table 2.1 outlines the 11 CROs that have been obtained, either by the Serious Fraud Office (SFO) or the Civil Recovery Unit (CRU). Table 2.2 summarises the four DPAs obtained to date by the SFO (note that DPAs are not yet available in Scotland).

---

[16] Criminal Justice Act 2003, s.22(3). The conditions may include a financial element: Criminal Justice Act 2003, s.23A. For further consideration of conditional cautions, see Robert A. Braddock, 'Rhetoric or Restoration? A Study into the Restorative Potential of the Conditional Cautioning Scheme', *International Journal of Police Science and Management* (2011), 13(3): 195.

[17] Ministry of Justice, *Code of Practice for Adult Conditional Cautions: Part 3 of the Criminal Justice Act 2003* (January 2013), para. 2.21 *et seq.*

[18] Criminal Justice Act 2003, s.24.

[19] Ministry of Justice, *Code of Practice for Adult Conditional Cautions: Part 3 of the Criminal Justice Act 2003* (January 2013), para. 2.7.

[20] CPS, *Adult Conditional Cautions (The Director's Guidance)* (7th ed, April 2013), para. 12.1.

Table 2.1 Civil recovery orders obtained by the SFO and CRU

Date	Agency	Business	Nature of case	Unlawful conduct	Self-report	Business advantage gained	Nature of order
October 2008	SFO	Balfour Beatty	Payment irregularities within a subsidiary company during a construction project in Egypt, which had been completed in 2001	These payments did not comply with requirements of accurate business records under section 221 of the Companies Act 1985	Yes	Linked to a $130 UNESCO construction joint venture	£2.25 million CRO, plus a contribution towards the costs of the proceedings
October 2009	SFO	AMEC plc	Receipt of irregular payments associated with a project of which AMEC was a shareholder	Failure to comply with the requirements of section 221 of the Companies Act 1985	Yes	Unspecified	£4,943,648 CRO plus the costs incurred
February 2011	SFO	MW Kellogg Ltd	Criminal activity by third parties (i.e. MWKL's parent company and others)	The SFO acknowledged 'that MWKL was used by the parent company and was not a willing participant in the corruption'[a]	Yes	Not specified. The amount in question related to share dividends from profits/revenues generated as a result of bribery and corruption by the third parties	£7,028,077 CRO

(continued)

Table 2.1 (continued)

Date	Agency	Business	Nature of case	Unlawful conduct	Self-report	Business advantage gained	Nature of order
April 2011	SFO	DePuy International Ltd	A DPA had been concluded with the US DoJ in relation to the same unlawful conduct, and the SFO were of the view that a criminal prosecution in the UK was precluded due to double jeopardy	Payments to intermediaries for the purpose of making corrupt payments to Greek medical officials	No (Referral came via US authorities)	Estimated to be approx. £14.8 million. Retention and enhancement of market position	£4.829 million CRO, plus prosecution costs. This figure took account of 'a global resolution' (including disgorgement and recovery in other jurisdictions)
July 2011	SFO	Macmillan Publishers Ltd	Allegations of bribery and corruption in relation to the supply of educational materials	Not specified beyond general allegations of bribery and corruption	No (Referral came via World Bank)	Contracts to supply products (educational materials) valued at approximately £11.2 m	£11,263,852.28 CRO, plus SFO costs of £27,000
January 2012	SFO	Mabey Engineering (Holdings) Ltd	Share dividends derived from contracts that had been won as a result of unlawful conduct. The contracts in question had been won by Mabey and Johnson, a subsidiary company	Included corruption and breaches of UN sanctions	Yes	Not specified. The amount in question related to share dividends from contracts that had been won as a result of unlawful conduct by a subsidiary company	£131,201 CRO, plus costs of £2440. The subsidiary company had previously been convicted, and this CRO was said to represent 'the conclusion of all matters related to the self-referral'[b]

Table 2.1 (continued)

Date	Agency	Business	Nature of case	Unlawful conduct	Self-report	Business advantage gained	Nature of order
July 2012	SFO	Oxford Publishing Ltd	OPL subsidiaries had offered and made payments, directly and through agents, intended to induce recipients to award competitive tenders and/or publishing contracts for schoolbooks	Bribery and/or corruption	Yes	Unspecified. The amount in question related to money received by wholly owned OPL subsidiaries as a result of unlawful conduct	£1,895,435 CRO, plus SFO costs of £12,500
November 2012	CRU	Abbott Group Ltd	Corrupt payments by a subsidiary company	Corrupt payments. No further details were specified, due to potential for future criminal investigations of others	Yes	Unspecified. The amount in question related to profit made by the company following a contract that had been entered into by one of its overseas subsidiaries. That subsidiary had made corrupt payments	£5.6 million CRO

(continued)

Table 2.1 (continued)

Date	Agency	Business	Nature of case	Unlawful conduct	Self-report	Business advantage gained	Nature of order
December 2014	CRU	International Tubular Services Ltd	Corrupt payments made by a former employee to secure additional contractual work	Not specified, beyond the making of corrupt payments	Yes	Not specified. The amount of the CRO represented the profit from the corrupt contract	£172,000 CRO
September 2015	CRU	Brand-Rex Ltd	Corrupt inducements by an associated person	Failure to prevent bribery, contrary to section 7 of the Bribery Act 2010	Yes	Not specified. The amount of the CRO was based on the company's gross profit from the unlawful activity	£212,800 CRO
April 2016	CRU	Braid Group (Holdings) Ltd	(1) Unauthorised Expenses incurred by an employee of a customer (2) A profit sharing arrangement with a Director of a customer company	Breach of sections 1 and 7 of the Bribery Act 2010	Yes	Not specified. The amount of the CRO represented the gross profit from the relevant contracts	£2.2 million CRO

[a]Cited in the Stolen Asset Recovery Initiative (StAR) Initiative Corruption Database 'Bonny Island Liquefied Natural Gas Bribe Scheme (TSKJ Consortium) / KBR – M.W. Kellogg Ltd', available at: https://star.worldbank.org/corruption-cases/node/20226 (last accessed October 20, 2017)
[b]Cited in the Stolen Asset Recovery Initiative (StAR) Initiative Corruption Database 'Mabey Engineering (Holdings) Ltd', available at: http://star.worldbank.org/corruption-cases/node/20233 (last accessed October 20, 2017)

2 NEGOTIATED JUSTICE AND ENFORCEMENT LEGITIMACY   21

Table 2.2 Deferred prosecution agreements obtained by the SFO[a]

Date	Agency	Business	Nature of case	Sanctioned offence	Self-report	Business advantage gained	Nature of DPA
November 2015	SFO	Standard Bank	Failure to prevent bribery by its sister company, Stanbic Bank Tanzania, to a local partner in Tanzania, Enterprise Growth Market Advisors (EGMA) to induce members of the Government of Tanzania	Failure of a commercial organisation to prevent bribery contrary to section 7 of the Bribery Act 2010	Yes	Gained favour for a proposal for a US$600 m [£398.8 m] private placement to be carried out on behalf of the Government of Tanzania. The placement generated transaction fees of US$8.4 m [£5.6 m], shared by Stanbic Tanzania and Standard Bank	DPA[b] with compensation of US$6 m plus interest of US$1,046,196.58; disgorgement of profit of US$8.4 m; payment of a financial penalty of US$16.8 m; and payment of costs incurred by the SFO (£330,000)
July 2016	SFO	Anonymous SME	Company's employees and agents involved in the systematic offer and/or payment of bribes to secure contracts in foreign jurisdictions	Conspiracy to corrupt, contrary to section 1 of the Criminal Law Act 1977, conspiracy to bribe, contrary to section 1 of the same Act, and failure to prevent bribery, contrary to section 7 of the Bribery Act 2010	Yes	The total gross profit from the implicated contracts amounted to £6,553,085	DPA with financial orders of £6,553,085: comprised of a £6,201,085 disgorgement of gross profits and a £352,000 financial penalty. (The SFO agreed not to seek costs.)

(continued)

Table 2.2 (continued)

Date	Agency	Business	Nature of case	Sanctioned offence	Self-report	Business advantage gained	Nature of DPA
January 2017	SFO	Rolls Royce plc	12 counts of conspiracy to corrupt, false accounting and failure to prevent bribery. The company, and its associated persons, used a network of agents to bribe officials in at least seven different countries	Six offences of Conspiracy to corrupt, contrary to section 1 of the Criminal Law Act 1977; Five offences of Failure of a commercial organisation to prevent bribery contrary to section 7(1)(b) of the Bribery Act 2010; and one offence of false accounting contrary to s. 17(1)(a) of the Theft Act 1968	No	Profit gained equated to £258,170,000	DPA with disgorgement of profit of £258,170,000, a financial penalty of £239,082,645, and payment of costs of £12,960,754
April 2017	SFO	Tesco Stores Limited	Accounting irregularities. Tesco overstated its profits by over £326 m between February and September 2014 in relation to how the company booked payments from its suppliers	TBC. Details of the DPA yet to be made publically available due to on-going prosecution of three Directors in relation to this case. Individuals charged with fraud by false accounting contrary to s17 Theft Act 1968 and fraud by abuse of position contrary to s1 and s4 Fraud Act 2006	TBC	TBC	TBC

[a]Adapted from Nicholas Lord and Mike Levi, 'In Pursuit of the Proceeds of Transnational Corporate Bribery: The UK Experience to Date', in Colin King, Clive Walker, and Jimmy Gurulé (eds), *The Handbook of Criminal and Terrorism Financing Law* (Palgrave, 2018)

[b]The SFO recorded the figures in US Dollars. The exchange rate on the day of the announcement (November 30, 2015) was US1$: £0.6646439742

Negotiated Justice and Legitimacy

'Legitimacy' remains a contested concept,[21] with different interpretations depending on the discipline. For the purposes of this book, we approach legitimacy from a criminological perspective. Since the 1990s, legitimacy has emerged as an established concept in criminological analysis and in the context of criminal justice.[22] It is a concept that implies questions of normative compliance with laws and rules, and the extent to which those being regulated and policed recognise those laws and enforcement authorities as being rightful and just. Nation states criminalise behaviours in part because they are recognised to be inherently 'bad'; there is a strong moral (and political) dimension to criminalisation. However, as with negotiated justice, little attention has been given to legitimacy in relation to white-collar and corporate crimes, albeit with a few notable exceptions.[23] In the context of corporate crime and negotiated justice, significant questions are raised in terms of how justice can be negotiated when there is no admission of guilt from implicated corporates. What are the implications for social fairness and moral/procedural equality if state authorities negotiate non-criminal sanctions with corporates for harmful, criminal behaviours in the absence of a guilty admission? How do we establish whether negotiated justice is a legitimate state response? This section lays the foundations of these questions.

What Is 'Legitimacy'?

Without legitimacy, enforcement approaches underpinned by 'negotiated justice' are likely to encounter problems. Without legitimacy,

---

[21] See W.B. Gallie, 'Essentially Contested Concepts', *Proceedings of the Aristotelian Society, New Series* (1956), 56: 167–198.

[22] Justice Tankebe and Alison Liebling, 'Legitimacy and Criminal Justice: An Introduction', in Justice Tankebe and Alison Liebling (eds), *Legitimacy and Criminal Justice: An International Exploration* (Oxford University Press, 2013).

[23] See Tom R. Tyler, 'Self-Regulatory Approaches to White-Collar Crime: The Importance of Legitimacy and Procedural Justice', in Sally S. Simpson and David Weisburd (eds), *The Criminology of White-Collar Crime* (Springer, 2009); Mike Levi, 'Legitimacy, Crimes and Compliance in "the City": *De Maximis non Curat Lex?*', in Justice Tankebe and Alison Liebling (eds), *Legitimacy and Criminal Justice: An International Exploration* (Oxford University Press, 2013).

people's attitudes and behaviours are likely to deviate from those desired. Without legitimacy, cooperation—a central feature of negotiation—is unlikely to be forthcoming. So legitimacy is important. Establishing legitimate enforcement responses is important as nation states are required to adequately pursue 'global corporate elites' that are engaging in criminal behaviours, such as transnational corporate bribery.[24] For instance, nation states must implement international frameworks for enforcement created by intergovernmental organisations such as the Organisation for Economic Co-operation and Development (OECD)[25] and the United Nations (UN).[26] These frameworks create pressures (e.g. of political, economic, legal, normative kind) for nation states to sign up to and implement key Conventions aimed at reducing harmful crimes and behaviours, such as bribery in business. How well nation states enforce these frameworks is scrutinised on a regular basis via peer-monitoring and evaluation,[27] though countries cannot be compelled to do something in response. But legitimacy must also be communicated not only to those companies that are to be regulated but also to the wider public. Without legitimacy, corporations are unlikely to cooperate with enforcement authorities (even with a view to negotiating an outcome to a criminal case, even where admissions of guilt may not be required). So how do we understand and analyse legitimacy? First, we need to consider three key issues:

i. what does 'legitimacy' actually mean?
ii. what does legitimacy, or illegitimacy, actually look like, and how is it accomplished under different conditions?
iii. for whom do enforcement responses need to be seen as legitimate and how do associated groups legitimate them?

---

[24] Nicholas Lord, 'Establishing Enforcement Legitimacy in the Pursuit of Rule-Breaking "Global Elites": The Case of Transnational Corporate Bribery', *Theoretical Criminology* (2016), 20(3): 376.

[25] OECD Convention on Combatting Bribery of Foreign Public Officials in International Business Transactions 1997.

[26] United Nations Convention Against Corruption 2003 (UNCAC).

[27] See, for example, OECD, *Implementing the OECD Anti-Bribery Convention: Phase 4 Report: United Kingdom* (OECD, 2017).

Legitimacy is a concept that derives from the Latin *legitimus*, meaning what is 'lawful, 'appropriate' or 'just'[28] and it is created through relational processes and interactions between those with power and authority (such as law enforcement authorities), and the responses of those who are subject to such authority and regulation (such as the business community). Legitimacy has been referred to as a '"slippery" concept to handle',[29] 'fragile'[30] and as a 'warm, fuzzy term'.[31] It can be defined both as a 'concept', where we can determine the basic meaning of the term 'legitimate' and delineate what we say about a particular enforcement response and whether we call it 'legitimate'; and as a 'conception', where we can specify criteria that need to be met by a rule or decision in order for it to actually be legitimate in the relevant sense.[32] For instance, there may be competing conceptions over whether a 'regulation' or 'crime-control' model of enforcement reflects legitimate norms.

A core theme in legitimacy research is the need for 'procedural justice'.[33] This literature indicates that if people view the behaviours, processes and procedures of the enforcement authorities as fair, they are more likely to be viewed as legitimate. This in turn enables established rules and corresponding enforcement decisions to be more willingly accepted and complied with. Correspondingly, legitimacy requires

---

[28] Justice Tankebe and Alison Liebling, 'Legitimacy and Criminal Justice: An Introduction', in Justice Tankebe and Alison Liebling (eds), *Legitimacy and Criminal Justice: An International Exploration* (Oxford University Press, 2013).

[29] Mike Hough, Jonathan Jackson, and Ben Bradford, 'Legitimacy, Trust and Compliance: An Empirical Test of Procedural Justice Theory Using the European Social Survey', in Justice Tankebe and Alison Liebling (eds), *Legitimacy and Criminal Justice: An International Exploration* (Oxford University Press, 2013), p. 330.

[30] Andrew Jefferson, 'The Situated Production of Legitimacy: Perspectives from the Global South', in Justice Tankebe and Alison Liebling (eds), *Legitimacy and Criminal Justice: An International Exploration* (Oxford University Press, 2013), p. 249.

[31] Mike Levi, 'Legitimacy, Crimes and Compliance in "the City": *De Maximis non Curat Lex?*', in Justice Tankebe and Alison Liebling (eds), *Legitimacy and Criminal Justice: An International Exploration* (Oxford University Press, 2013).

[32] Wilfried Hinsch, 'Legitimacy and Justice: A Conceptual and Functional Clarification', in Jorg Kühnelt (ed.), *Political Legitimization Without Morality?* (Springer, 2008), p. 39.

[33] See Tom R. Tyler, 'Public Trust and Confidence in Legal Authorities: What Do Majority and Minority Group Members Want from the Law and Legal Authorities?', *Behavioral Sciences and the Law* (2001), 19: 215; Tom R. Tyler, 'Psychological Perspectives on Legitimacy and Legitimation', *Annual Review of Psychology* (2006), 57: 375.

both a normative and empirical dimension. At a normative level, we can assess whether there are agreed standards of what is right and good and whether they are justifiable; at an empirical level we can assess whether the rules and procedures are acknowledged as rightful by those being regulated, even if personal standards are not met.[34] Analysing both is needed to understand the legitimacy of enforcement authorities and their responses.[35] Normatively, we can seek to identify 'objective' criteria, that reflect our values and expectations, for assessing the legitimacy of any given arrangement.[36] For example, we might investigate whether a particular institutional enforcement arrangement meets certain essential requirements of 'legitimacy', such as being procedurally just, fair and transparent, irrespective of whether the people being regulated believe they meet them or not. Given our focus here on serious corporate financial crimes we might ask, for example, whether the SFO is normatively legitimate and has moral standing, rather than simply report empirically that some of those being regulated (i.e. businesses, individuals etc.) *believe* it to have moral standing. In these terms, empirical legitimacy is more an observation of the subjective beliefs of regulated or otherwise relevant communities that demonstrate (or not) approval of the SFO, its authority and power to enforce, and this can ensure commensurability between these different groups. In addressing such issues then, we can gain insight into why exactly people cooperate with enforcement authorities for reasons beyond self-interest that reflect shared social motivations.[37] This does not imply any evaluative or normative commitment on behalf of those observers who use it to describe social order.[38]

---

[34] See Wilfried Hinsch, 'Legitimacy and Justice: A Conceptual and Functional Clarification', in Jorg Kühnelt (ed.), *Political Legitimization Without Morality?* (Springer, 2008); David Beetham, *The Legitimation of Power* (2nd ed, Palgrave Macmillan, 2013).

[35] See Anthony Bottoms, and Justice Tankebe, 'Beyond Procedural Justice: A Dialogic Approach to Legitimacy in Criminal Justice', *Journal of Criminal Law and Criminology* (2012), 102(1): 119.

[36] Wilfried Hinsch, 'Legitimacy and Justice: A Conceptual and Functional Clarification', in Jorg Kühnelt (ed.), *Political Legitimization Without Morality?* (Springer, 2008).

[37] Tom R. Tyler, *Why People Cooperate: The Role of Social Motivations* (Princeton University Press, 2011).

[38] Wilfried Hinsch, 'Legitimacy and Justice: A Conceptual and Functional Clarification', in Jorg Kühnelt (ed.), *Political Legitimization Without Morality?* (Springer, 2008).

There are, however, normative limits as to what we, as social scientists, should empirically describe as legitimate.[39]
Legitimacy also comprises both a *process* of justification and an *outcome* as justified.[40] However, establishing and justifying the processes and outcomes of 'legitimate' enforcement is diverse and complex given that legitimacy is both an 'output' of multiple influences, such as ideology, conformism or interests, and an 'input', as it shapes how we behave.[41] In this sense, there are dialogic, relational and interactive processes central to establishing legitimacy.[42] In other words, it is important to understand how different stakeholders perceive who or what is legitimate, or illegitimate, and how their related perceptions legitimate or de-legitimate enforcement responses—these processes and stakeholder responses are contextual and situated[43] and shaped by the tensions between law and morality in any 'institutional normative order'.[44] Furthermore, we can also distinguish between the necessary and contingent aspects of legitimacy across different jurisdictions.[45] For instance, varying contexts of legitimacy, such as the legal, institutional, political and economic

[39] Anthony Bottoms, and Justice Tankebe, 'Beyond Procedural Justice: A Dialogic Approach to Legitimacy in Criminal Justice', *Journal of Criminal Law and Criminology* (2012), 102(1): 119.

[40] Susanne Karstedt, 'Trusting Authorities: Legitimacy, Trust, and Collaboration in Non-democratic Regimes', in Justice Tankebe and Alison Liebling (eds), *Legitimacy and Criminal Justice: An International Exploration* (Oxford University Press, 2013), emphases in original.

[41] Mike Levi, 'Legitimacy, Crimes and Compliance in "the City": De Maximis non Curat Lex?', in Justice Tankebe and Alison Liebling (eds), *Legitimacy and Criminal Justice: An International Exploration* (Oxford University Press, 2013).

[42] Anthony Bottoms, and Justice Tankebe, 'Beyond Procedural Justice: A Dialogic Approach to Legitimacy in Criminal Justice', *Journal of Criminal Law and Criminology* (2012), 102(1): 119.

[43] Andrew Jefferson, 'The Situated Production of Legitimacy: Perspectives from the Global South', in Justice Tankebe and Alison Liebling (eds), *Legitimacy and Criminal Justice: An International Exploration* (Oxford University Press, 2013), p. 249.

[44] Anthony Bottoms, and Justice Tankebe, 'Beyond Procedural Justice: A Dialogic Approach to Legitimacy in Criminal Justice', *Journal of Criminal Law and Criminology* (2012), 102(1): 119, 156–159; Neil MacCormick, *Institutions of Law: An Essay in Legal Theory* (Oxford University Press, 2007).

[45] Nicholas Lord, 'Establishing Enforcement Legitimacy in the Pursuit of Rule-Breaking "Global Elites": The Case of Transnational Corporate Bribery', *Theoretical Criminology* (2016), 20(3): 376.

conditions and landscapes, are always contingent, shaped by particular geographical and historical developments. Different mixtures of these contingent contexts create conditions that are more, or less, conducive to legitimate enforcement (e.g. conforming to international norms), and therefore shape whether there is more, or less, legitimacy of the enforcement responses. That said, it is possible to identify certain minimum normative criteria that must necessarily be evident for enforcement to be legitimate in these contexts.[46] Throughout this book, and in our analysis of CROs and DPAs, we revisit these features of legitimacy in the context of all of the so-called 'settlements' to date, and consider the factors that shape whether these mechanisms can be described as legitimate. We draw on our expertise of researching in the areas of white-collar and corporate crimes, and identify key normative issues in these approaches.

Applying the Construct of 'Legitimacy' to 'Negotiated Justice'

But what does legitimacy look like in practice and how is it established and maintained? The literature on legitimacy, and legitimate power, frequently outlines three key features prominent to the concept,[47] which we draw upon to understand the connections between legitimacy and 'negotiated justice':

1. *Legality* (rule conformity): the acquiring (rightful authority) and exercising (due performance) of power in line with established rules, legislation and standards that permeate from the international level (e.g. international anti-corruption conventions) to the domestic level (i.e. implementing legislation);
2. *Normative validity*: the justifiability of established rules and the enforcing of these by responsible authorities that meet societally accepted standards of rightful authorization and due performance in line with certain shared moral, ethical and just values and standards; and,

---

[46] Ibid.

[47] For a useful threefold framework for thinking through legitimate power, see David Beetham, *The Legitimation of Power* (2nd ed, Palgrave Macmillan, 2013). We draw on this framework here to inform our analysis.

3. *Legitimation* (through performative actions): the (empirically evidenced) actions of relevant groups (i.e. businesses involved in international commerce, international NGOs, the 'regulated') which recognise, acknowledge and serve to confirm the authority of those in power (i.e. enforcement authorities).

In these terms, 'legitimacy' as an analytical construct can be applied, both empirically and normatively, to the negotiation of justice in cases of corporate crimes. Thus, it is important to analyse whether negotiated justice meets certain objective, value-laden criteria or standards or norms of what is right and good and whether these standards are clarified and justified. That is our focus in this book. It is also important to analyse, empirically, whether negotiated justice is acknowledged as rightful by the beliefs and actions of stakeholders. As noted in chapter one, we were driven to write this book as the landscape—particularly with DPAs—is developing; our focus then is a normative critique, rather than on empirical research. Thus, while we do not draw upon our own empirical research in our discussion, it is hoped that others will take up this challenge and that this book will provide a foundation for future research to explore legitimacy from an empirical perspective.

Before proceeding further, it is worth briefly saying a bit more about legitimacy and 'legality', 'normative validity', and 'legitimation'.

The Legality of 'Negotiated Justice'

In terms of legality, there are two primary questions:

- Is 'negotiated justice' supported by a sound legal foundation and guided by established rules?
- Is the power of enforcement authorities to engage in the negotiation of justice validly acquired and properly exercised in accordance with well-established standards?

If the answer to these questions is 'no', then we might argue that negotiated justice in cases of corporate crimes are *illegitimate*. However, legality and rules alone cannot provide a fully adequate criterion of legitimacy as established rules aren't simply justified because they are rules[48]—they

---

[48] See David Beetham, *The Legitimation of Power* (2nd ed, Palgrave Macmillan, 2013).

require justification by reference to considerations which lie beyond them, and this requires consideration of how (or whether) such rules and mechanisms are justified and grounded in line with the norms, standards and expectations of affected populations, like the business community as well as the general public.

The Normative Validity of 'Negotiated Justice'
The key question here is one of justifying rules in line with shared cultural norms and beliefs. So we need to ask whether the rules and standards that guide negotiated justice meet societally accepted standards? Does the underlying principle or rationale of negotiated justice reflect commonly accepted beliefs about what justice should look like in relation to corporate crimes? Are those with the power to engage in negotiated justice properly qualified (i.e. in the sense of formal qualification, expertise and experience) to exercise their use? Do their actions meet levels of expected performance?[49]

If these conditions are not met, then a *legitimacy deficit* may emerge. However, do such shared beliefs extend beyond the regulator and the regulatee? There is an argument that negotiated justice is an example of the differential treatment afforded to white-collar and corporate criminals when contrasted with 'conventional', 'ordinary' criminals, which raises questions of social fairness and equality before the law as well as accusations of 'cheque-book justice'. Thus, it might be argued that there is a need to revisit enforcement responses, with the aim of ensuring equality before the law and that corporates cannot simply buy their way out of prosecution.[50] Alternatively, it might be argued that there is work to be done in order to communicate to the wider public how 'justice' is (apparently) accomplished in relation to complex financial crimes and why this sometimes differs to conventional crime.

---

[49] A further issue here is how to measure expected performance. Should that be assessed from the perspective of enforcement authorities? What, however, if (parts of) the general public express different views—though it is acknowledged that there are significant difficulties in measuring such public opinion. For some sentiments on this issue, see, for example, Larry Elliott, 'Gordon Brown: Bankers Should Have Been Jailed for Role in Financial Crisis', *The Guardian* (October 31, 2017); J.R., 'The Economist Explains: Why Have So Few Bankers Gone to Jail?', *The Economist* (May 14, 2013); Ian Birrell, 'Iceland Has Jailed 26 Bankers, Why Won't We?', *The Independent* (November 15, 2015).

[50] See Nicola Padfield, 'Deferred Prosecution Agreements', *Archbold Review* (2012), 7: 4.

The Legitimation of 'Negotiated Justice'
Finally, while processes and beliefs relating to negotiated justice may conform to established rules and be in line with the accepted standards of justice and rationality, legitimacy is properly determined by the actions of relevant groups. This is an empirical matter. The key, and possibly the most important, question is whether the actions of the regulated communities and other relevant groups (and the public)—such as corporates implicated in corresponding criminal cases or NGOs with an interest in addressing financial crimes—recognise, acknowledge and serve to confirm the authority of those with the power to be able to engage in negotiated justice.

Public recognition and acknowledgement enhances legitimacy. If this recognition is not evident, or if it is withdrawn, then *delegitimation* can occur. Establishing legitimacy in the context of competing agendas and competing policy imperatives is important for the functioning of criminal justice given that different stakeholders need to 'buy-into' and 'legitimate' rules, enforcement policies and the exercising of power. Those 'qualified' to legitimate enforcement responses are incredibly varied.[51] For example, we can delineate between a broad array of stakeholders: politicians, regulators, domestic prosecutors, financial services, the judiciary and those involved in the criminal justice process, the regulated, victims (both corporate and individual), the media, the general public, and given the global nature of economic activity also consumers, investors, overseas employees, competitors and international regulators/prosecutors.

Establishing the preferred response to corporate crimes that each of these groups would like to see is problematic as governments may act in contradictory ways. In one sense, they might want to do as little as possible, so as not to stifle enterprise and foreign investment, or lose corporations as providers of tax and employment. This would also save on the high costs of prosecution. In another sense, they might also want to (appear to) act tough so as to communicate the impression that they are not protecting a minority of (global) elites and in doing so meet international expectations. There is a fine line between enterprise that is praised and rewarded, and economic crime that reveals a dark side of capitalism.

---

[51] See Mike Levi, 'Legitimacy, Crimes and Compliance in "the City": *De Maximis Non Curat Lex?*', in Justice Tankebe and Alison Liebling (eds), *Legitimacy and Criminal Justice: An International Exploration* (Oxford University Press, 2013).

CHAPTER 3

Civil Recovery Orders: Law, Policy and Practice

Abstract This chapter explores the development of civil recovery as an enforcement tool in the context of corporate crime. It explores the preference for 'civil settlement', with the consequence that corporate wrongdoers can avoid criminal prosecution. A number of concerns are explored in this regard. This chapter also examines the divergent approaches of the Serious Fraud Office and the Scottish Civil Recovery Unit, namely that as the rest of the UK moves away from CROs, such powers remain an important cog in the Scottish enforcement response to corporate crime.

Keywords Corporate crime · Civil recovery · Civil settlement · Transparency · Serious Fraud Office · Civil Recovery Unit

Civil recovery orders (CROs) are provided for in the Proceeds of Crime Act 2002 (POCA),[1] enabling an enforcement authority to bring a proprietary action to target the proceeds of criminal activity. Civil recovery does not require criminal conviction; indeed for some that is its most

---

[1] The civil recovery provisions came into force on February 24, 2003: SI 2003/120 The Proceeds of Crime Act 2002 (Commencement No. 4, Transitional Provisions and Savings) Order 2003.

© The Author(s) 2018
C. King and N. Lord, *Negotiated Justice and Corporate Crime*, Crime Prevention and Security Management,
https://doi.org/10.1007/978-3-319-78562-2_3

pressing attraction.[2] Others, however, have been critical, particularly in relation to undermining procedural protections of the criminal process.[3] Indeed, it has been argued that 'the use of a civil process to target criminal assets in the absence of criminal conviction is an affront to legitimacy'.[4]

In the context of corporate wrongdoing, the Serious Fraud Office (SFO) first used its civil recovery powers in October 2008 (Balfour Beatty), while the Scottish Civil Recovery Unit (CRU) obtained its first CRO in 2012 (Abbott Group Ltd). With the advent of deferred prosecution agreements (DPAs) in England and Wales (see Chapter 4), it is to be expected that civil recovery actions will not be as prevalent in responding to corporate crime, though the SFO does still have the power to pursue such actions. As DPAs are not yet available in Scotland, it is now more likely to see CROs (in the corporate context) being used within the Scottish system rather than elsewhere in the UK. It is noticeable though that only four CROs, related to corporate wrongdoing, have been obtained by the CRU. The extent to which we will continue to see such powers being used in the corporate context is not clear, particularly if Scotland does adopt suggestions that it should legislate for DPAs to bring it in line with the rest of the UK.[5]

As will be seen below, there have only been 11 CROs against corporates from 2008 to the end of 2017. Notwithstanding the low numbers, it is worthwhile considering the use of CROs not least as such powers are still used by the CRU today (and are still available to the SFO),

---

[2] For consideration of arguments in favour of civil recovery, see Anthony Kennedy, 'Justifying the Civil Recovery of Criminal Proceeds', *Journal of Financial Crime* (2004), 12(1): 8. See also Colin Nicholls, Timothy Daniel, Alan Bacarese, and John Hatchard, *Corruption and Misuse of Public Office* (2nd ed, Oxford University Press, 2011), p. 255 *et seq.*

[3] See, generally, Michelle Gallant, *Money Laundering and the Proceeds of Crime: Economic Crime and Civil Remedies* (Edward Elgar, 2005). See also Liz Campbell, 'The Recovery of "Criminal" Assets in New Zealand, Ireland and England: Fighting Organised and Serious Crime in the "Civil" Realm', *Victoria University Wellington Law Review* (2010), 41: 15; John Lea, 'Hitting Criminals Where It Hurts: Organised Crime and the Erosion of Due Process', *Cambrian Law Review* (2004), 35: 81.

[4] Jennifer Hendry and Colin King, 'How Far is Too Far? Theorising Non-Conviction-Based Asset Forfeiture', *International Journal of Law in Context* (2015), 11(4): 398, 407.

[5] OECD, *Implementing the OECD Anti-Bribery Convention. Phase 4 Report: United Kingdom* (OECD, 2017), p. 59.

but also because these cases (with both the SFO and the CRU) reinforce the emphasis on negotiation and non-contention between corporates/regulators over the past decade. Indeed, 'since the civil recovery component of the settlement will be, in essence, a private one, then, in principle, everything, including the publicity, is negotiable'.[6] Throughout, it is important to consider whether the use of CROs, as non-criminal law sanctioning mechanisms, can be viewed as a legitimate approach to dealing with corporates implicated in serious financial crimes. At the outset, it must be recognised that civil recovery powers are legislated for under POCA, thus these powers have been validly enacted by the political system. However, as set out in Chapter 2, legality and rules alone cannot provide a fully adequate criterion of legitimacy; rules are not simply justified because they are rules.[7] Indeed, it has been argued elsewhere that the reliance upon civil law mechanisms such as CROs—where criminal prosecution is arguably more appropriate—lacks legitimacy.[8] In the context of corporate crime, our discussion focuses on how CROs became a substitute for criminal prosecution due to difficulties inherent in criminal enforcement in the corporate context. The effect of this emphasis on reaching a settlement was to enable corporates to negotiate their way *out* of the criminal process. More specifically, we consider how enforcement agencies have demonstrated a preference for settlement, rather than criminal prosecution. We then explore each of the CROs obtained to date to illustrate how that preference varied under the leadership of different SFO directors as well as in Scotland. Third, we engage with the role of self-reporting in the process of negotiation. Next, we outline the role of 'global settlements' and how they have been received by the judiciary, with emphasis on the *Innospec* case. Fifth, it is important to consider what happens to seized assets, particularly problems related to incentivisation. Finally, we conclude by examining the role of transparency in CROs to date.

---

[6] Peter Alldridge, 'Bribery and the Changing Pattern of Criminal Prosecution', in Jeremy Horder and Peter Alldridge (eds), *Modern Bribery Law: Comparative Perspectives* (Cambridge University Press, 2013), p. 247.

[7] See David Beetham, *The Legitimation of Power* (2nd ed, Palgrave Macmillan, 2013). See also Ota Weinberger, 'Legal Validity, Acceptance of Law, Legitimacy: Some Critical Comments and Constructive Proposals', *Ratio Juris* (1999), 12(4): 336.

[8] Jennifer Hendry and Colin King, 'Expediency, Legitimacy, and the Rule of Law: A Systems Perspective on Civil/Criminal Procedural Hybrids', *Criminal Law and Philosophy* (2017), 11(4): 733.

A Preference for Settlement?

Up until 2012 the SFO had an explicit policy of settling self-reported foreign bribery[9] cases 'civilly wherever possible' without also pursing criminal prosecution.[10] As Alldridge notes, 'It was not the objective to litigate every case. As with any other civil case, a settlement will often be the preferred outcome'.[11] The preference for civil settlements has, however, been criticised.[12] Thomas LJ was particularly scathing in the *Innospec* case:

> Those who commit such serious crimes as corruption of senior foreign government officials must not be viewed or treated in any different way to other criminals. It will therefore rarely be appropriate for criminal conduct by a company to be dealt with by means of a civil recovery order … It is of the greatest public interest that the serious criminality of any, including companies, who engage in the corruption of foreign governments, is made patent for all to see by the imposition of criminal and not civil sanctions. It would be inconsistent with basic principles of justice for the criminality of corporations to be glossed over by a civil as opposed to a criminal sanction.[13]

Such sentiments underpin the argument in this chapter that CROs undermine legitimacy in those cases where serious criminal conduct is known to have occurred. The remarks of Thomas LJ raise questions over the performance of enforcement authorities when criminal behaviours are dealt with through non-criminal responses—enforcement powers are

---

[9] All eleven CROs involve allegations of bribery and/or corruption, so our focus is primarily on such wrongdoing.

[10] SFO, *Approach of the Serious Fraud Office to Dealing with Overseas Corruption* (July 2009). The explicit emphasis on settling such self-report cases 'civilly wherever possible' was removed in 2012. See Debevoise and Plimpton LLP, *Client Update: Serious Fraud Offices Issues New Policies on Self-Reporting, Facilitation Payments and Business Expenditures* (October 12, 2012).

[11] Peter Alldridge, 'Civil Recovery in England and Wales: An Appraisal', in Colin King, Clive Walker, and Jimmy Gurulé (eds), *The Handbook of Criminal and Terrorism Financing Law* (Palgrave, 2018), p. 516.

[12] See OECD, *Phase 3 Report on Implementing the OECD Anti-Bribery Convention in the United Kingdom* (March 2012), p. 33.

[13] *R v Innospec Limited*, Sentencing Remarks, Crown Court at Southwark, March 26, 2010, Thomas LJ, para. 38.

not being exercised in accordance with fundamental legal principles, such as equal treatment before the law. Moreover, the move towards a policy of civil remedies was a product of obstacles to criminal law enforcement. Taking 2002 as a point of departure (i.e. the year that POCA was signed into law and also the year that foreign bribery was criminalised in the UK): Robert Wardle (SFO Director 2003–2008) initially pursued a strategy of 'command and control' but achieved zero prosecutions. He was constrained by various factors, some practical and pragmatic,[14] and others ideological.[15] Wardle recognised the need for legal, strategic and operation reform. Consequently, 'while rules were established and publicly supported, a "deficit" emerged as enforcement "performance" was inadequate and the "rightful authority" of the SFO was undermined by political interference which in turn undermined legitimacy'.[16]

Thus, when Richard Alderman took over as SFO Director (2008–2012), there was a significant change in strategy as negotiated justice through settling civilly with corporates implicated in bribery became the default response.[17] The benefits to corporate wrongdoers were clear, namely enabling cases to be dealt with on more favourable terms and eliminating the prospect of criminal prosecution for the wrongdoing in question. It also provided a degree of consistency and certainty to the enforcement strategy, despite underlying questions around the legitimacy of concluding criminal cases through civil means. Alderman's time as SFO Director, however, has not been widely lauded and, indeed, his preference for civil settlement whilst Director subsequently impacted upon his position as a member of an OECD advisory group on bribery and anti-corruption.[18]

---

[14] Such as an inadequate legal framework and difficulties in obtaining evidence overseas.

[15] Such as political interference by the executive (the BAE Systems case was the epitome of this). These issues are developed further in Chapter 6.

[16] Nicholas Lord, 'Establishing Enforcement Legitimacy in the Pursuit of Rule-Breaking "Global Elites": The Case of Transnational Corporate Bribery', *Theoretical Criminology* (2016), 20(3): 376, 398. See also David Leigh, 'The Fall Guy', *The Guardian* (April 18, 2008).

[17] See SFO, *Approach of the Serious Fraud Office to Dealing with Overseas Corruption* (July 2009).

[18] Fraudwatch, Alderman Forced to Leave OECD Advisory Group, May 7, 2015, available at: https://fraudwatchonline.com/index.php/news/briberyandcorruption/3480-alderman-forced-to-leave-oecd-advisory-group (last accessed January 19, 2018).

Under the regime of David Green (2012–2018), there has been a notable shift in the discourse and rhetoric towards a hard-line prosecutorial stance.[19] Indeed, there was initially some skepticism as to how he would approach CROs. That concern was somewhat dispelled shortly after Green took up his post (April 2012), with the completion of the Oxford Publishing Ltd CRO (July 2012) (discussed below). Noticeably, though, shortly thereafter the SFO preference for settling foreign bribery cases was discontinued (October 2012), and the SFO has not since entered into any CROs. More recently, the introduction of DPAs has enabled Green to adopt what has been described as a hybrid approach to enforcement.[20] Green is due to step down as SFO Director in April 2018; at the time of writing, his successor has not yet been named.

Interestingly, the use of CROs in the corporate context began in Scotland just as the SFO moved away from such an enforcement response. Thus, CROs continue to be used as a means for corporates to negotiate out of criminal prosecution. With the advent of DPAs, it might have been expected that CROs, in the corporate context, would no longer be used however that is not the case. As shall be seen in Chapter 4, Scotland has not adopted DPAs, thus CROs remain the primary enforcement response for certain criminal offences, particularly transnational corporate bribery.

We now turn to consider the orders that have been granted.

Experiences to Date

The Alderman Years (2008–2012)

In 2008, the SFO obtained its first CRO. The background to that order concerned payment irregularities within a subsidiary of **Balfour Beatty**, during a construction project to rebuild the Alexandria Library in Egypt. Balfour Beatty self-reported these irregularities, and subsequently agreed to admit to a failure to comply with requirements of accurate business records under section 221 of the Companies Act 1985. The Consent Order[21] was for the amount of £2.25 million, plus a contribution

---

[19] See Tim Harvey, 'Man on a Mission', *Fraud Magazine*, November/December 2013.
[20] DPAs are discussed in Chapters 4 and 5.
[21] Provision for 'Consent Orders' is contained in POCA, s.276(1).

towards the costs of the proceedings.[22] Given the value of the contract, there has been criticism in relation to the amount of the CRO and how that amount was calculated.[23]

The next CRO obtained by the SFO was against **AMEC plc**. Similar to Balfour Beatty, this Consent Order related to a failure to comply with requirements of section 221 of the Companies Act 1985. AMEC self-reported the receipt of irregular payments, and a Consent Order was made for the amount of £4,943,648, plus the (unspecified) costs involved of the proceedings.[24]

The third CRO obtained by the SFO was against **MW Kellogg Ltd**. This order related to criminal activity by third parties (i.e. MWKL's parent company and others). The SFO recognised that MWKL took no part in the criminal activity which generated the funds, and that the company did self-refer the matter to the SFO and cooperated with the subsequent investigation. The CRO was in the amount of £7,028,077, which represented money that the company was due to receive as share dividends from profits/revenues generated as a result of bribery and corruption by the third parties. The SFO acknowledged 'that MWKL was used by the parent company and was not a willing participant in the corruption'.[25]

The next CRO concerned payments to intermediaries for the purpose of making corrupt payments to Greek medical officials. The corporate benefit sought from these corrupt payments was retention and enhancement of market position for the company—**DePuy International Ltd** (a UK subsidiary of Johnson and Johnson). This issue was referred to

---

[22] See the Stolen Asset Recovery Initiative (StAR) Corruption Database 'Balfour Beatty Plc', available at: http://star.worldbank.org/corruption-cases/node/19833 (last accessed October 20, 2017).

[23] See Transparency International (UK), *Deterring and Punishing Corporate Bribery: An Evaluation of UK Corporate Plea Agreements and Civil Recovery in Overseas Bribery Cases* (Transparency International, 2012), p. 65.

[24] See the Stolen Asset Recovery Initiative (StAR) Corruption Database 'AMEC plc', available at: http://star.worldbank.org/corruption-cases/node/19815 (last accessed October 20, 2017). It has been suggested that the construction project in question was the Incheon Bridge in Korea: Simon Bowers, Amec and Serious Fraud Office settle $9 million "irregular receipts" case, *The Guardian* (October 26, 2009).

[25] Cited in the Stolen Asset Recovery Initiative (StAR) Corruption Database 'Bonny Island Liquefied Natural Gas Bribe Scheme (TSKJ Consortium)/KBR—M.W. Kellogg Ltd', available at: https://star.worldbank.org/corruption-cases/node/20226 (last accessed October 20, 2017).

the SFO by US authorities, who had concluded a DPA with DePuy's parent company in relation to the same unlawful conduct. The SFO was of the view that a criminal prosecution in the UK was precluded on the grounds of double jeopardy, and that the most appropriate sanction was a CRO. Of the sales tainted by the unlawful conduct, approximately £14.8 million was thought to have passed to DePuy International Ltd and this amount was said to represent 'unlawfully obtained property'. A CRO was granted against DePuy International Ltd for the amount of £4.829 million, plus (unspecified) prosecution costs. It was said that this amount took account of 'a global resolution' (including disgorgement and recovery in other jurisdictions for the same underlying unlawful conduct).[26] Again here, however, there has been criticism that 'the basis of the calculation is not clear'.[27]

MacMillan Publishers Ltd was the next company subjected to a CRO, following allegations of bribery and corruption in relation to the supply of educational materials. These allegations were referred to the SFO by the World Bank.[28] The SFO (in cooperation with the City of London Police and the World Bank) selected three jurisdictions[29] and required the company's external lawyers to conduct detailed investigations into all public tender contracts during the period 2002–2009. The SFO concluded: 'It was impossible to be sure that the awards of tender to the Company in the three jurisdictions were not accompanied by a corrupt relationship'. A CRO was granted for the amount of £11,263,852.28, plus SFO costs of £27,000.[30]

The next CRO obtained by the SFO was against **Mabey Engineerings (Holdings) Ltd**. This order came about following a self-referral by a subsidiary company (Mabey and Johnson), which was

---

[26] Cited in the Stolen Asset Recovery Initiative (StAR) Corruption Database 'Johnson & Johnson/DePuy International Ltd (UK subsidiary)', available at: http://star.worldbank.org/corruption-cases/node/20234 (last accessed October 20, 2017).

[27] Transparency International (UK), *Deterring and Punishing Corporate Bribery: An Evaluation of UK Corporate Plea Agreements and Civil Recovery in Overseas Bribery Cases* (Transparency International, 2012), p. 65.

[28] In a negotiated resolution, in April 2010, MacMillan Limited was debarred from World Bank contracts for a period of six years.

[29] Namely Rwanda, Uganda, and Zambia.

[30] Cited in the Stolen Asset Recovery Initiative (StAR) Corruption Database 'MacMillan Publishers Limited', available at: http://star.worldbank.org/corruption-cases/node/20100 (last accessed October 20, 2017).

subsequently convicted of foreign bribery. A settlement was agreed with the parent company, as shareholder, for the amount of £131,201 (plus costs of £2440) in recognition of sums received through share dividends derived from contracts that had been won as a result of that unlawful conduct of the subsidiary company. The CRO was said to represent 'the conclusion of all matters related to the self-referral' following the successful criminal prosecution of the company and former company officers.[31]

This CRO has been described as a 'landmark development in anti-corruption enforcement'.[32] It attracted extensive criticism for many reasons including: the parent company did not know about the subsidiary's unlawful conduct (which was acknowledged by the SFO); questions as to whether it is appropriate to target shareholders who may not have access to information indicating unlawful conduct; and whether it is possible for institutional shareholders to micromanage companies.[33] The SFO was unmoved by such criticisms, however. As the then-SFO Director, Richard Alderman, stated:

> shareholders who receive the proceeds of crime can expect civil action against them to recover the money. The SFO will pursue this approach vigorously. In this particular case, however, the shareholder was totally unaware of any inappropriate behaviour. The company and the various stakeholders across the group have worked very constructively with the SFO to resolve the situation, and we are very happy to acknowledge this. The second, broader point is that shareholders and investors in companies are obliged to satisfy themselves with the business practices of the companies they invest in. This is very important and we cannot emphasise it enough. It is particularly so for institutional investors who have the knowledge and expertise to do it. The SFO intends to use the civil recovery process to pursue investors who have benefitted from illegal activity.

---

[31] See the Stolen Asset Recovery Initiative (StAR) Corruption Database 'Mabey Engineering (Holdings) Ltd', available at: http://star.worldbank.org/corruption-cases/node/20233 (last accessed October 20, 2017).

[32] J. Pickworth and C. Lee, *Dechert On Point—Special Alert* (January 2012), available at: https://www.dechert.com/files/Publication/1d9cdaa5-638d-4c9b-b0f5-865899aa38b8/Presentation/PublicationAttachment/d203cec1-b012-4e93-90fb-8a552c9e58af/White_Collar_SA_01-12_SFO_Recovers.pdf (last accessed October 20, 2017).

[33] See, for example, C. Binham and K. Burgess, 'Investors alarmed by SFO warning', *Financial Times*, January 12, 2012.

Where issues arise, we will be much less sympathetic to institutional investors whose due diligence has clearly been lax in this respect.[34]

Significant concerns exist, however, in relation to the above CROs. Most notably, there is concern as to how the amount of the CRO is calculated.[35] Not everyone agrees with such criticism. For example, it has been suggested (in relation to the Balfour Beatty CRO) that: 'The relatively low value of the civil recovery was a reflection of the company's cooperation, its willingness to enter into new internal control mechanisms, and the fact that neither the company nor any individual obtained a commercial advantage from the conduct'.[36] Such suggestions, however, are open to debate. If anything, it might be argued that that CRO was unduly favourable to the corporate: not only did the corporate avoid the threat of criminal prosecution (and the possibility of debarment and loss of reputation if convicted), it is not clear whether the CRO did in fact entail full disgorgement of profits from the contract. Even if so, there are additional financial benefits to corporates arising from, say, bribery (e.g. reputation accruing from a particular project; increased market share) that ought also be taken into consideration. Again, the lack of transparency is notable—it is not possible to say what factors were taken into account when deciding upon the amount of the CROs above. Indeed, there is a complete lack of transparency in relation to all CROs that were entered into during Alderman's reign. (This lack of transparency is discussed below.)

The Green Years (2012–2018)

The most recent CRO obtained by the SFO was in July 2012 against **Oxford Publishing Ltd** (OPL). Indeed, this is the only corporate CRO

---

[34] Cited in FCPA Compliance Report, *The SFO Speaks in the Mabey & Johnson Case: Private Equity – Are You Listening?* available at: http://fcpacompliancereport.com/2012/01/the-sfo-speaks-in-the-mabey-johnson-case-private-equity-are-you-listening/ (last accessed July 28, 2017).

[35] See Transparency International (UK), *Deterring and Punishing Corporate Bribery: An Evaluation of UK Corporate Plea Agreements and Civil Recovery in Overseas Bribery Cases* (Transparency International, 2012), p. 65.

[36] Colin Nicholls, Timothy Daniel, Alan Bacarese, and John Hatchard, *Corruption and Misuse of Public Office* (2nd ed, Oxford University Press, 2011), p. 218.

that was entered into under the reign of David Green.[37] In announcing the OPL consent order, the SFO acknowledged previous criticism as to a lack of transparency in civil recovery matters. This case, then, was the first time that the CRO and Claim were made public.[38] The CRO was for the amount of £1,895,435 (plus £12,500 costs), relating to money received by OPL subsidiaries—namely Oxford University Press East Africa (OUPEA) and Oxford University Press Tanzania (OUPT)—as a result of unlawful conduct, namely bribery and/or corruption. The SFO investigation came about following a self-referral from Oxford University Press (OUP),[39] and the costs of that investigation were met by OUP. The investigation concluded 'that OUPEA and OUPT had offered and made payments, directly and through agents, intended to induce the recipients to award competitive tenders and/or publishing contracts for schoolbooks to OUPEA and OUPT'.[40] As these are wholly owned subsidiaries, OPL would have received money derived from the unlawful conduct. Thus, the SFO conducted an accounting examination to determine the benefit from the tainted contracts and to determine the appropriate amount to be recovered. It is worth mentioning that no allowance was made for the bribes or inducement payments.

The SFO press release detailed a number of reasons as to why a CRO was sought instead of criminal prosecution. These reasons include:

1. The test under the Code for Crown Prosecutors was not met, and there was no likelihood that it would be met in future. This view was based on factors including (i) key material was not in an evidentially admissible format for criminal prosecution and (ii) witnesses for a prosecution were based overseas and were considered unlikely to assist or cooperate with a UK criminal investigation.

---

[37] The SFO has pursued CROs against individuals, related to financial wrongdoing involving corporates, such as in the case of Griffiths Energy International Inc. For background to that case, see *SFO v Saleh* [2015] EWHC 2119 (QB).

[38] SFO Press Release, Oxford Publishing Ltd to Pay Almost £1.9 Million as Settlement After Admitting Unlawful Conduct in Its East African Operations (July 3, 2012).

[39] OUP made a separate self-referral to the World Bank, as two of the tenders in question were funded by the World Bank. As part of a Negotiated Resolution Agreement between OUP and the World Bank, OUPEA and OUPT were debarred for three years while OUP received a conditional non-debarment.

[40] SFO Press Release, Oxford Publishing Ltd to Pay Almost £1.9 Million as Settlement After Admitting Unlawful Conduct in Its East African Operations (July 3, 2012).

2. Difficulties in relation to obtaining evidence from the jurisdictions involved and potential risks to affected persons.
3. OUP satisfied the criteria set out in the SFO guidance on self-reporting matters of overseas corruption.
4. There was no evidence of Board level knowledge or connivance within OUP in relation to the conduct at issue.
5. The products supplied were of a good standard and were provided at open market values.
6. The resources needed to facilitate an investigation were considerable. It was thought that civil recovery would be 'a better strategic deployment of resources to other investigations which have a higher probability of leading to a criminal prosecution'.
7. All gross profit from tainted contracts will be disgorged.
8. The subsidiaries will be subject to parallel World Bank procedures, and will be debarred from future World Bank tenders for a number of years.

The SFO acknowledged that OUP unilaterally offered to contribute £2 million to not-for-profit organisations in sub-Saharan Africa.[41] However, the SFO decided that that offer should not be included in the terms of the CRO 'as the SFO considers it is not its function to become involved in voluntary payments of this kind'.[42] Commenting on the CRO the SFO Director, David Green, stated:

> This settlement demonstrates that there are, in appropriate cases, clear and sensible solutions available to those who self report issues of this kind to the authorities. The use of Civil Recovery powers has been exercised in accordance with the Attorney General's guidelines. The company will be adopting new business practices to prevent a recurrence of these issues and these new procedures will be subject to an extensive and detailed review.[43]

The OPL CRO does address concerns expressed in relation to the lack of transparency that existed with earlier CROs. Indeed, as we shall see

---

[41] According to the press release, 'This was a reflection of the seriousness with which OUP views the course of events that were subject to the investigation and a wish to acknowledge that the conduct of OUPEA and OUPT fell short of that expected within its wider organisation'. Ibid.
[42] Ibid.
[43] Ibid.

in Chapter 4, this emphasis on transparency would carry through to the DPA regime. That notwithstanding, there remains the question 'whether justice that is negotiated is commensurate with fundamental democratic legal principles, whether the negotiations are carried out in public or not'.[44] Moreover, there remain concerns that CROs continue to be used as an alternative to criminal prosecution,[45] enabling corporates to negotiate their way out of prosecution as well as providing an excuse (or motivation) for the SFO not to pursue investigations (particularly difficult ones, as here) when an alternative (non-criminal) option is available. While corporates might well be receptive to settling cases of criminal wrongdoing by means of a CRO,[46] it is not apparent that the general public would condone such settlements.

Although obtained in July 2012, the OPL CRO remains the most recent CRO obtained by the SFO. That, however, may be due to the adoption of DPAs, which were provided for in the Crime and Courts Act 2013.

Scottish Experiences

As the SFO moved away from the use of CROs, particularly in light of criticism (discussed below) from the OECD,[47] HMCPSI,[48] and others (such as Transparency international),[49] we witness a different approach in Scotland—where CROs are now being used in the context of corporate crime (again here, particularly in transnational bribery cases). In Scotland, to mark the coming into force of the Bribery Act 2010

---

[44] Donald R. Cressey, 'Negotiated Justice', *Criminology* (1968), 5(4): 5, 9.

[45] Though it is recognised that the SFO noted that the Code for Crown Prosecutors was not met in this instance.

[46] See, for example, Barry Vitou and Richard Kovalevsky, 'When It Comes to Corporate Crime—in the Whitehall Corridors of Power: The Fight Is on', available at: http://thebriberyact.com/2011/02/21/when-it-comes-to-corporate-crime-in-the-whitehall-corridors-of-power-the-fight-is-on/ (last accessed January 18, 2018).

[47] OECD, *Phase 3 Report on Implementing the OECD Anti-Bribery Convention in the United Kingdom* (March 2012).

[48] HM Crown Prosecution Service Inspectorate (HMCPSI), *Report to the Attorney General on the Inspection of the Serious Fraud Office* (November 2012).

[49] Transparency International (UK), *Deterring and Punishing Corporate Bribery: An Evaluation of UK Corporate Plea Agreements and Civil Recovery in Overseas Bribery Cases* (Transparency International, 2012).

(on July 1, 2011) an initiative was approved whereby businesses could self-report bribery offences 'with a view to consideration being given by the Crown to refraining from prosecuting the business and referring the case to the Civil Recovery Unit (CRU) for civil settlement'.[50] This initiative is reviewed annually, and is currently scheduled to operate until June 2018.[51] In this section, we briefly outline the four Scottish corporate CROs to date; again here, the same considerations of legitimacy arise.

The first CRO obtained by the Scottish CRU was against **Abbot Group Ltd**. The company self-reported that corrupt payments had been made by an overseas subsidiary. The sum to be paid represented the profit made by the company under the contract entered into by its subsidiary and an overseas oil and gas company. Abbot was the first company to enter into a civil settlement under the bribery and corruption self-reporting initiative for businesses that had been introduced in 2011.[52] The company had self-reported to the COPFS, but it was deemed that the case should be forwarded to the CRU for an extra-judicial settlement. The Scottish self-reporting initiative has been said to mirror the former approach of the SFO, i.e. the preference for settling cases civilly where possible.[53]

The next CRO obtained by the CRU was against **International Tubular Services Ltd** (ITS). There is little information about this case, though the facts are relatively straightforward to summarise: ITS benefited from corrupt payments that had been made by a former employee to secure additional contractual work from a customer in Kazakhstan. These corrupt payments came to light when the company was being sold, and a self-report was made. The CRO was for the amount of £172,000, representing the profit from the corrupt contract.

---

[50] COPFS, *Guidance on the Approach of the Crown Office and Procurator Fiscal Service to Reporting by Businesses of Bribery Offences* (June 2017), para. 1.

[51] There is no indication what factors influence whether the self-reporting initiative will be continued or otherwise during this annual review.

[52] Civil Recovery Unit, *Civil Recovery Unit Annual Report 2012/13* (Scottish Government), p. 9.

[53] John Hull and Dan Smith, *The Future of Civil Settlements in Criminal Matters* (Latham & Watkins, In Practice, April 2013), available at: https://www.lw.com/thought-Leadership/The-Future-of-Civil-Settlements-in-Criminal-Matters (last accessed November 3, 2017). See also Gordon Kaiser, 'Corruption in the Energy Sector: Criminal Fines, Civil Judgments and Lost Arbitrations', *Energy Law Journal* (2013), 34(1): 193, 237.

More significant is the case of **Brand-Rex Ltd**—the first (known) case enforcing section 7 of the Bribery Act. This case thus merits further discussion. At issue here was a failure to prevent bribery by an associated third party. The company had operated an incentive scheme ('Brand Breaks') whereby distributors and installers would receive rewards for meeting or exceeding sale targets. While the incentive scheme was itself legitimate, problems arose when an independent installer (an associated person) offered rewards that would be due to him under the scheme to an employee of a customer. As that employee was in a position to influence decisions, Brand-Rex was thus in breach of section 7 of the Bribery Act.[54] Brand-Rex self-reported to the COPFS, and the case was dealt with by the CRU. The speed of resolution is noticeable: the self-report was made in June 2015 and the CRO was granted in September of the same year. The CRO was for the amount of £212,800, based on the amount of the company's gross profit from the unlawful activity.[55]

As noted earlier, the Scottish self-reporting initiative (introduced in 2011) mirrors the former approach of the SFO—which was discontinued in 2012.[56] If a case such as Brand-Rex were to arise in England and Wales (E + W), it is now likely that a DPA would be the preferred route for the SFO. Certainly, it is unlikely that a CRO would be pursued in such a case: as has been pointed out 'Although civil recovery orders are available in England, the SFO no longer considers them appropriate save in exceptional cases'.[57] What, though, would constitute an exceptional case is not immediately clear. A final point to mention here is how the different approaches in E + W and Scotland might influence

---

[54] Note, the company did not assert that its anti-bribery and corruption policies were adequate—which would have provided a complete defence.

[55] See Jody Harrison, Firm Pays Fine After Reporting Itself to Crown Office, *The Herald* (September 25, 2015); Laura Forde, *Failing to Prevent Bribery—Prevention Is Better than Cure*, DLA Piper Regulatory Update (October 13, 2015).

[56] While CROs went against Green's hard-line prosecutorial stance, it must be recognised that he re-iterated on numerous occasions the importance of self-reporting (e.g. David Green, *Speech at the Inaugural Fraud Lawyers Association*, March 26, 2013). Indeed, self-reporting remains an important consideration for the SFO under the new DPA regime implemented in 2013 (see Chapter 4).

[57] Johanna Walsh, Lessons Learned from the First Resolution Under s7 of the Bribery Act, *Kingsley Napley Criminal Law Blog* (October 6, 2015), available at: https://www.kingsleynapley.co.uk/insights/blogs/criminal-law-blog/lessons-learned-from-the-first-resolution-under-s7-of-the-bribery-act (last accessed November 3, 2017).

a corporate's decisions to self-report. Of course forum-shopping will not be well perceived, but 'any company with significant operations in Scotland should carefully consider whether the Scottish Crown Office would be the more appropriate recipient of a self-report'.[58]

The most recent CRO obtained by Scottish authorities was against **Braid Group (Holdings) Ltd**. Due to potential further criminal proceedings against individuals involved, the details that were made public are rather brief. In short, the company made a self-report to the COPFS in relation to two breaches of the Bribery Act. The first of these related to an agreement between a company employee and an employee of a customer. An account was used for unauthorised expenses to be incurred by the latter, including personal travel, holidays, hotels, and more. The second breach concerned a profit sharing arrangement with a Director of a customer company, whereby profit on services provided to the customer was split in return for orders continuing to be placed with Braid. The company accepted that there was a contravention of sections 1 and 7 of the Bribery Act.[59] A CRO was granted for the amount of £2.2 million, which represented the gross profit made from the relevant contracts.[60]

Given that Scotland has adopted a self-reporting initiative similar to that of the SFO during Alderman's reign, it is unsurprising that many

---

[58] See Debevoise and Plimpton LLP, 'UK "Corporate Offence"—Scottish Company Enters First Settlement Expressly Relating to Section 7 of the Bribery Act', *FCPA Update* (October 2015, vol. 7, no. 3), p. 15.

[59] It is also worth noting that, on the basis of his knowledge of, and involvement in, a bribery arrangement a court order was granted for the purchase of shares held by a director of the company. That director only received 'par value' for his shareholding—which was approximately £18 million less than the actual value of his shareholding: *In the petition of Nigel Gray and ors, for Orders pursuant to sections 994 and 996 of the Companies Act 2006 in respect of Braid Group (Holdings) Ltd* [2015] CSOH 146, para. 161. This decision was upheld on appeal: *In the Reclaiming Motion of Nigel Anthony Harden Gray and ors, for Orders pursuant to sections 994 and 996 of the Companies Act 2006 in respect of Braid Group (Holdings) Ltd* [2016] CSIH 68. See also *In the cause of Nigel Anthony* Harden Gray against Braid Logistics (UK) Ltd [2017] CSOH 44.

[60] The CRU press release is reproduced on 'thebriberyact.com' website: Barry Vitou and Richard Kovalevsky, 'Civil Settlement for Scottish Company which self-reported violations of section 1 & section 7 of the Bribery Act highlights difference of approach North of the Border', available at: http://thebriberyact.com/2016/04/17/civil-settlement-for-scottish-company-which-self-reported-violations-of-section-1-section-7-of-the-bribery-act-highlights-difference-of-approach-north-of-the-border/ (last accessed November 6, 2017).

of the same criticisms arise again here. First, there are concerns that CROs are being used as an alternative to criminal prosecution, in situations where prosecution is arguably more appropriate. Indeed, the OECD Phase Four evaluation noted that Scotland has 'never in practice applied criminal liability to a legal person for foreign bribery or similar misconduct'.[61] Second, this approach can give rise to the perception that corporates are able to buy their way out of criminal prosecution and punishment. Third, and on a related point, while the monetary amount of the CROs does disgorge the profits from the tainted contracts, there is no additional monetary penalty. Moreover, the CRO does not take account of any other benefits, such as enhanced reputation as a result of being involved in a particular project or the possibility of increasing, or consolidating, market share by virtue of being involved in a particular project (even if the profits from that project are subsequently disgorged). Fourth, while some—albeit limited—information is available in the Scottish press releases, there is concern as to a lack of transparency (discussed below).

Self-Reporting

It is worth saying a bit more about self-reporting, given the current Scottish initiative as well as the previous SFO approach to self-reporting (and acknowledging that self-reports are still encouraged by the SFO, not least in relation to DPAs). Self-reporting is a clear example of how the process of *negotiation* can result in corporates avoiding criminal prosecution. In essence, self-reporting encourages corporates to volunteer information to the authorities in the hope of (quick[62]) civil settlement. Again, we see benefits to both the corporate (e.g. avoidance of prosecution; a more favourable settlement) and law enforcement authorities (e.g. enhancing efficiency by allowing resources to be used elsewhere; avoiding lengthy, drawn-out investigations; certainty in the enforcement strategy, including avoiding the risk of acquittal at trial). Yet, the core

---

[61] OECD, *Implementing the OECD Anti-Bribery Convention: Phase 4 Report: United Kingdom* (OECD, 2017), para. 152.

[62] The Scottish Guidance envisages a speedy process, with an initial evaluation from SOCU expected within 8 weeks of the self-report: see COPFS, *Guidance on the Approach of the Crown Office and Procurator Fiscal Service to Reporting by Businesses of Bribery Offences* (June 2017), para. 13.

criticism remains that, in essence, the emphasis on settlement (from both the SFO and CRU) has enabled corporates to negotiate their way *out* of the criminal process and the perception is that they are buying their way out of prosecution. In this section we outline details of the Scottish self-reporting initiative.

While the COPFS initiative is distinct from that previously operated by the SFO, there have been discussions between the COPFS and the SFO and there will be liaison between them about self-reported cases. This is particularly relevant where a business makes a report to, say, the SFO but that report relates to conduct in, or predominantly in, Scotland. In such a situation, the SFO will refer the business to the Scottish authorities. The reverse also applies, i.e. the COPFS will refer a business to the SFO if it receives a report that relates to conduct in, or predominantly in, England and Wales.[63] Where there are cross-border issues, each case will be considered on its own merits. Factors that will influence whether a report should be made to the SFO or the COPFS include: whether the headquarters or registered office is located in either Scotland or E + W; where the business predominantly carries on its business; and whether the wrongdoing at issue has taken place in either Scotland or E + W.[64]

A self-report under the COPFS initiative should be made to the Serious and Organised Crime Unit (SOCU) of the COPFS. This report must be made by a solicitor acting on behalf of the business. There are minimum requirements before a self-report will be accepted by the SOCU, namely that the business: (1) has conducted a thorough investigation (which may include assessment by forensic accountants), must be willing to share any resulting report with SOCU, and must acknowledge that the report is being provided to SOCU on its behalf; (2) agrees

---

[63] Ibid., para. 4.

[64] See Ibid., para. 5. In practice, however, there are practical difficulties. For example, in 2014 an MOU was signed between various law enforcement agencies (namely COLP, COPFS, CPS, FCA, MDP, NCA, and SFO) establishing new rules for assigning foreign bribery cases. A separate MOU was also signed between the COPFS and the SFO setting out further rules for co-ordination and co-operation between those agencies. However, during the 2017 OECD Phase Four evaluation, 'Representatives of the Scottish police and prosecuting authorities were unfortunately not aware of the existence of the 2014 MOUs and how they affect the attribution of foreign bribery cases between the SFO and Scottish authorities'. OECD, *Implementing the OECD Anti-Bribery Convention: Phase 4 Report: United Kingdom* (OECD, 2017), para. 75.

to disclose to SOCU the full extent of criminal conduct that has been discovered; (3) describes what has been done to prevent a repetition of the conduct; and (4) is committed to meaningful dialogue with the Crown.[65]

While SOCU staff will be willing to enter into early discussions with a solicitor acting on behalf of a business, and will be prepared to provide information about how cases will be dealt with, they will not enter discussions without the identity of the business being disclosed. Information, including the initial report, will be recorded. While it will be treated in confidence, that information can be used in any subsequent criminal investigation/prosecution or in any civil recovery investigation. The information may also be shared with prosecution or law enforcement agencies in other jurisdictions.[66] The business will be asked to acknowledge that the information it provides can be used in this manner. The business must be clear that the report is made on behalf of the Board or the Partners, as appropriate, and that the business has received legal advice before making the report or disclosing information to the Crown.[67]

It is important to note that reports will only be accepted from businesses, and not from individuals. If an individual wishes to make a report without the knowledge of the business, that falls outside the self-reporting initiative.[68]

In deciding whether a self-reported case should be passed to the CRU, with a view to civil settlement, the following criteria will be taken into account:

- the nature and seriousness of the offence and the extent of the harm caused;
- the extent of the wrongdoing within the business, including whether conduct was authorised by, or connived in, by senior management, or restricted to a small number of lower-ranking individuals;

---

[65] COPFS, *Guidance on the Approach of the Crown Office and Procurator Fiscal Service to Reporting by Businesses of Bribery Offences* (June 2017), para. 7.
[66] Ibid., para. 8.
[67] Ibid., para. 9.
[68] Ibid.

- whether it is clear that the business is taking action as soon as the matter comes to the attention of senior management (as opposed to taking no action until it becomes aware that there is a risk that the conduct is going to come to light);
- whether the business (or the individuals involved in the matter reported) has any previous record for this type of conduct. This would go beyond a previous criminal conviction, and would include any regulatory enforcement action or warning;
- whether the individuals involved in the wrongdoing have left the business and, where decisions were taken at Board level, whether there is a new Board in place, and in both cases the timing and reasons for the departure of these individuals;
- whether the business has honoured its commitment to engage with the Crown meaningfully and in particular to disclose the full extent of the wrongdoing;
- whether the business had in place adequate anti-bribery systems at the time of the criminal conduct and whether it has further addressed this following the conduct;
- whether there are particular considerations which may weigh against prosecution, such as the consequences of prosecution for the company's employees and stakeholders.[69]

Each case will be considered on its own merits. Not all self-reported cases will be deemed suitable for civil settlement, for example there may be an overriding public interest in prosecution.[70]

Where a case is deemed suitable for referral to the CRU, an investigation under Part 5 of POCA will commence. This investigation may involve instructing a third party forensic accountancy firm[71] (the costs

---

[69] Ibid., para. 10.

[70] Ibid. In such cases, 'it is envisaged that the business will continue to cooperate with law enforcement. ... The business will be able to rely on their self-reporting and co-operation with the Crown and law enforcement as significant mitigating factors to be taken into account by the Court' (ibid., para. 10).

[71] The CRU may dispense with the requirement to instruct a third party forensic accountancy firm, for example where the business has submitted a forensic accountancy report as part of the self-report. This will be determined on a case-by-case basis. Ibid., para. 22.

of which will be borne by the self-reporting business).[72] If the business is obstructive to the forensic accountants (e.g. failure to allow access to accounting records) then the case will be returned to SOCU. If further criminality is uncovered by the forensic accountants, the case will also be returned to SOCU. In such circumstances, the case will only be re-referred to the CRU if SOCU is satisfied that there is good reason not to begin a criminal investigation.[73]

The CRU will use the final report from the forensic accountants 'to quantify the appropriate level of a settlement by reference to the property which has been obtained by the business through unlawful conduct'.[74] At this point, SOCU will be invited to formally intimate that no prosecution will be brought in relation to the conduct at issue subject to the full implementation of the settlement.[75] It is envisaged that any such settlement will be made public, unless there is a 'compelling reason' for confidentiality.[76]

'GLOBAL SETTLEMENTS': THE INNOSPEC AGREEMENT

Facts

The *Innospec* case is of importance in that it involved what was described as 'a global settlement' for wrongdoing in different jurisdictions.[77] A CRO and a confiscation order were envisaged as part of an agreement between the SFO and the company. The court, however, rejected the structure of the agreement, instead preferring to impose a fine (albeit for the same amount as had been agreed). This case is significant, not least

---

[72] Ibid., para. 15. The Guidance later states: 'The costs incurred by the business in respect of the forensic accountants may be taken into account when determining the appropriate level of any extra-judicial settlement but there should be no expectation by the business that these costs will be taken into account in every case' (ibid., para. 21).

[73] Ibid., para. 18.

[74] Ibid., para. 19.

[75] Ibid.

[76] Ibid., para. 20.

[77] For further discussion of Innospec and 'global settlements', see Polly Sprenger, *Deferred Prosecution Agreements: The Law and Practice of Negotiated Corporate Criminal Penalties* (Sweet and Maxwell, 2015), pp. 501–506. Sprenger notes that 'the term global is something of a misnomer'; indeed, global settlements have been used even where only one jurisdiction is affected (ibid., p. 499).

in that it demonstrated judicial discontent to act as a rubber-stamp for settlements negotiated by enforcement agencies. The emphasis on the role of the judiciary has subsequently been reflected in the DPA framework, where judicial oversight is a key provision.

It is worth, briefly, outlining the facts. Innospec Ltd is a UK company and a wholly owned subsidiary of Innospec Inc (a Delaware company, although its executive offices were based in the UK). At issue in this case were allegations of corruption in Indonesia and Iraq. The corruption in Indonesia was organised by the 'directing minds' of Innospec Ltd (the UK company), and involved 'systematic and large-scale corruption of senior Government officials'.[78]

From July 2005, US authorities[79] began investigations into Innospec Inc. The SFO was notified in October 2007, and its investigation began in May 2008. These investigations also revealed that bribes had been paid in relation to the UN Oil for Food Programme for Iraq, as well as with Iraq government officials after that programme had ended. Further, the investigations also revealed that Innospec had sold fuel additives to Cuba, in violation of US embargo regulations.

The Innospec investigations were carried out with the full cooperation of the independent directors of Innospec, who were of the view that they should admit criminal offences. In September 2008 discussions began with US authorities with a view to achieving 'a global settlement', and the SFO became party to those discussions.

Reaching a Global Settlement

The company entered into discussions with US authorities and the SFO, where much of the discussion focused on the financial position of Innospec Inc (the Delaware company) and its subsidiaries, and significantly its ability to pay. The authorities agreed that the fines and other penalties that might be imposed could exceed US$400 million in the US and US$150 million in the UK, which would exceed the company's ability to pay and continue trading. The authorities agreed that—in light of the company's admissions and co-operation—they would not

---

[78] *R v Innospec Limited*, Sentencing Remarks, Crown Court at Southwark, March 26, 2010, Thomas LJ, para. 4.

[79] Including the Department of Justice (DOJ), the Securities and Exchange Commission (SEC), and the Office of Foreign Asset Control (OFAC).

seek to impose a penalty that would drive the company out of business. Ultimately a settlement was proposed by the company that was acceptable to the US and UK authorities—subject to the approval of the courts in both the US and UK.

There were also discussions between the SFO and the US DOJ about the allocation of any such settlement. It was agreed that the SFO would have primacy in relation to the Indonesian corruption and the DOJ in relation to the Iraq corruption.[80] While the SFO initially proposed a 50:50 split, the DOJ rejected this and proposed a split of approximately 1/3 to the DOJ, 1/3 to the SFO, and 1/3 to the SEC and OFAC, which the SFO agreed to. The SFO share would be $12.7 million.

Following further discussion between the SFO and the company, it was agreed that the company would plead guilty to conspiracy to corrupt contrary to section 1 of the Criminal Law Act 1977. It was also agreed[81] that the amount to be paid would consist of a $6.7 million confiscation order to be imposed in the Crown Court and a $6 million CRO.[82] The plea agreements were then put forward for court approval. The agreement was approved in the US,[83] however in the UK Thomas LJ expressed some concerns as to the extent of the SFO's power to enter into such an agreement as well as the role of the courts in sentencing.[84]

Specifically, it was emphasised that 'the SFO cannot enter into an agreement under the laws of England and Wales with an offender as to the penalty in respect of the offence charged'.[85] Thomas LJ referred to 'the constitutional principle that, save in minor matters such as motoring offences, the imposition of a sentence is a matter for the judiciary'.[86] He continued:

---

[80] Although the Iraq corruption could have been prosecuted in the UK, the SFO had adopted the view that the most logical approach was to split the criminal liability of Innospec Inc and Innospec Ltd in this manner.

[81] 'It was accepted that it was for the court to determine the appropriate sentence, but the parties submitted that the approach upon which they were agreed should commend itself to the court as it was compatible with the approach being adopted in the US'. *R v Innospec Limited*, Sentencing Remarks, Crown Court at Southwark, March 26, 2010, Thomas LJ, para. 17.

[82] These would equate to £4.4 million (confiscation order) and £3.9 million (CRO) using the exchange rate on the day in question.

[83] See *Innospec*, paras. 18–20.

[84] See *Innospec*, paras. 23–28.

[85] *Innospec*, para. 26.

[86] *Innospec*, para. 27.

Principles of transparent and open justice require a court sitting in public itself first to determine by a hearing in open court the extent of the criminal conduct on which the offender has entered the plea and then, on the basis of its determination as to the conduct, the appropriate sentence. It is in the public interest, particularly in relation to the crime of corruption, that although, in accordance with the Practice Direction, there may be discussion and agreement as to the basis of plea, a court must rigorously scrutinise in open court in the interests of transparency and good governance the basis of that plea and to see whether it reflects the public interest.[87]

Thus, 'Agreements and submissions of the type put forward in this case can have no effect'.[88]

Approach to Sentencing

Thomas LJ expressed some sentiments about the approach to be adopted in sentencing. While our focus in this chapter is on civil recovery, it is useful to consider the approach enunciated by the court, specifically concerning fines, confiscation, and civil recovery. In relation to fines, Thomas LJ started by emphasising that 'corruption of foreign government officials or foreign government ministers is at the top end of serious corporate offending both in terms of culpability and harm'.[89] It was also noted that courts should impose penalties appropriate to the serious level of criminality involved. He referred to the US approach of imposing substantial fines, and in this case (in relation to the Iraq corruption) the minimum range would have been $101.5 million, plus disgorgement of profits.[90] He favoured consistency in financial penalties imposed in different jurisdictions:

> there is every reason for states to adopt a uniform approach to financial penalties for corruption of foreign government officials so that the penalties in each country do not discriminate either favourably or unfavourably against a company in a particular state. If the penalties in one state are lower than in another, businesses in the state with lower penalties will not be deterred so effectively from engaging in corruption in foreign states,

---

[87] *Innospec*, para. 27.
[88] *Innospec*, para. 28.
[89] *Innospec*, para. 30.
[90] *Innospec*, para. 31.

whilst businesses in states where the penalties are higher may complain that they are disadvantaged in foreign states.[91]

Thomas LJ continued to state that fines in corruption cases 'must be effective, proportionate and be dissuasive in the sense of having a deterrent element'.[92] His starting point, then, was that a fine comparable to that imposed in the US would be the starting point, and that this fine would be separate from depriving the company of the benefits obtained from the criminality.[93]

In relation to confiscation, it was noted that (under the applicable law in this case, namely the Criminal Justice Act) where the prosecutor gives written notice to the court that it would be appropriate to make a confiscation order, then confiscation would take primacy over a fine. If a company was able to pay both a fine and a confiscation order, then it would be expected to pay both. In *Innospec*, the benefits of the corrupt conduct were not only the profits from the contracts concerned but the contracts themselves—thus the benefit was said to be potentially as high as $160 million.[94]

In this instance, the Director of the SFO accepted that the court should determine whether to impose a fine in preference to a confiscation order. Thomas LJ explained the preference for a fine as follows:

> It is very important in the public interest and as a signal of deterrence to others that a fine of very considerable magnitude is imposed and is seen to be imposed as a mark of the serious criminal conduct of which the company is guilty. The offending itself must be severely punished quite irrespective of whether it has produced a benefit. The deprivation of any benefits obtained follows, as no person can be allowed to retain the benefit of his criminal conduct, but that is simply an additional consequence.[95]

Moreover, there would have been a conflict of interest if the Director had opted for confiscation given that the SFO would have been in line to share a portion of any monies realised by a confiscation order (this will be discussed in the next section).

---

[91] *Innospec*, para. 31.
[92] *Innospec*, para. 32.
[93] Ibid.
[94] *Innospec*, para. 34.
[95] *Innospec*, para. 36.

The court then turned to consider civil recovery. Thomas LJ was critical of the reasons advanced for the consent CRO in this case[96]: first, as criminal proceedings in relation to corruption in Iraq had been taken in the US, authorities believed that criminal proceedings in the UK for the same conduct would breach double jeopardy principles; they desired to mark such conduct by a penalty in the UK given that that is where the conduct had been organised. As the Iraqi criminality was punished by a fine of $14.1 million in the US courts, Thomas LJ deemed it inappropriate that the confiscation order in relation to the Indonesia corruption (which was the subject of UK proceedings) would thus be reduced, as 'the corruption in relation to Indonesia was at least as serious as that in respect of Iraq'. Second, Thomas LJ noted that compensation was to be paid in respect of Iraq, but no compensation was contemplated in respect of the Indonesia corruption.[97] Third, while payments were contingent upon future earnings of the company, Thomas LJ stated that that is no impediment to a fine.

Thomas LJ went on to emphasise what he described as a more important general principle. While part of this statement has been mentioned at the outset of this chapter, it is worthwhile repeating it more fully at this point:

> Those who commit such serious crimes as corruption of senior foreign government officials must not be viewed or treated in any different way to other criminals. It will therefore rarely be appropriate for criminal conduct by a company to be dealt with by means of a civil recovery order ... It is of the greatest public interest that the serious criminality of any, including companies, who engage in the corruption of foreign governments, is made patent for all to see by the imposition of criminal and not civil sanctions. It would be inconsistent with basic principles of justice for the criminality of corporations to be glossed over by a civil as opposed to a criminal sanction. There may, of course, be a place for a civil order, for example, as a means of compensation in addition to a fine. It is therefore plainly desirable that

---

[96] See *Innospec*, para. 37.

[97] As Thomas LJ stated: 'it is difficult to see why no compensation was being paid in respect of the corruption in Indonesia which was charged and punished in the UK, whilst paying compensation in respect of the corruption in Iraq which was charged and punished in the US'. *Innospec*, para. 37.

the Lord Chief Justice should consider directions that ensure any civil penalties are heard in conjunction with criminal proceedings.[98]

Sentence

Under the terms of the agreement proposed by the SFO and the company, the amount of $12.7 million (the SFO share of the global settlement) would consist of a a $6.7 million confiscation order and a $6 million CRO. As noted above, Thomas LJ had a clear preference that a fine be imposed. However, he was of the view that 'a fine of $12.7 million would have been wholly inadequate as a fine to reflect the criminality displayed by Innospec Ltd. This was corruption involving the payment of very substantial amounts to the most senior officials of the government of Indonesia over a long period of time'.[99] That notwithstanding, as he had indicated at an earlier hearing (albeit 'with considerable reluctance'[100]), he imposed a fine of $12.7 million once the US courts had approved the US plea agreement. He did stress, though, that were he not so limited then the fine would have been substantially higher ('the fine would have been measured in tens of millions'[101]).

Given that a fine was imposed for the amount of $12.7 million, 'There are no further funds available either for a compensation order, a civil recovery order or prosecution costs'.[102] A compliance and monitoring agreement was also put in place. Thomas LJ also stated:

> unless I had been satisfied that the new management of the company would not engage in similar conduct in the future, I would not have assented to a fine or other penalty that would have enabled the continuing survival of this company. If a company cannot pay the applicable fine without becoming insolvent, then it is for that company to show that the

---

[98] *Innospec*, para. 38.

[99] *Innospec*, para. 40. This view did take account of the fact that (1) the company would be entitled to credit for its early guilty plea and its cooperation with the investigation and (2) the management had changed and that an enhanced compliance programme was put in place.

[100] *Innospec*, para. 42.

[101] *Innospec*, para. 41.

[102] *Innospec*, para. 47.

new management has put that past behind them and will not engage in criminality in the future.[103]

Judicial Criticism of the Agreement

Notwithstanding his obvious distaste for the terms of the agreement, Thomas LJ stated that 'in all the circumstances and given the protracted period of time in which the agreement had been hammered out, I do not think it would have been fair to impose a penalty greater than that'.[104] He continued on to say:

> on this occasion, it would neither be just nor fair in the unusual circumstances of this case for this court to impose a penalty greater than the amount allocated to the UK. ... this court was placed in a position where it had little alternative but to agree to the limit of $12.7m, if it was to avoid injustice.[105]

He did stress, however, that:

> the circumstances of this case are unique. There will be no reason for any such limitation in any other case and the court will not consider itself in any way restricted in its powers by any such agreement.[106]

Thomas LJ went on to emphasise that not only is an agreement between prosecutors outwith the powers of the Director of the SFO, but also that any such agreement 'cannot be in accordance with basic constitutional principles'.[107] He further criticised the agreement on the grounds that it lacked principle:

> The gravamen of the criminality was centred in the UK, the criminality of the corruption in Indonesia was no less serious than that in Iraq and there was no reason to prefer compensation to Iraq over compensation to both

---

[103] *Innospec*, para. 49.

[104] *Innospec*, para. 42.

[105] Ibid. The court also referred to the decision in *R v Whittle & Others* [2008] EWCA Crim 2560.

[106] *Innospec*, para. 42.

[107] *Innospec*, para. 43.

Iraq and Indonesia. My provisional view is that the amount should have been divided 50:50.[108]

While Thomas LJ did commend the Director of the SFO for his determined pursuit of corruption, such as in this case, he did send a note of warning: 'the Director of the SFO had no power to enter into the arrangements made and no such arrangements should be made again'.[109]

What Happens to Realised Money?

In England and Wales, the Asset Recovery Incentivisation Scheme (ARIS) operates to allocate a percentage (up to 50%)[110] of any assets realised under POCA to agencies involved in investigations/prosecutions. Thus, controversially, agencies involved in civil recovery proceedings can 'share' in any realised assets. The ARIS was introduced in 2006, following concern that proceeds of crime powers were not being sufficiently used. The SFO participated in ARIS until 2014, however that is no longer the case. Since April 2014, the SFO instead receives a fixed sum in lieu, which amounts to the cost of running the SFO Proceeds of Crime Unit.[111]

While there is nothing to indicate that the SFO was influenced by this monetary incentive (when it did participate in ARIS), such incentivisation schemes have been heavily criticised on the grounds that they skew policing priorities and lead to 'policing for profit'.[112] Indeed, in *Innospec*, Thomas LJ recognised the potential for 'a very considerable conflict of

---

[108] *Innospec*, para. 43.

[109] *Innospec*, para. 45.

[110] The other 50% goes to the Home Office.

[111] Home Office, *Asset Recovery Statistical Bulletin 2011/12–2016/17*. Statistical Bulletin 15/17 (September 2017), p. 9.

[112] See, for example, Dick M. Carpenter, Lisa Knepper, Angela C. Erickson, and Jennifer McDonald, *Policing for Profit: The Abuse of Civil Asset Forfeiture* (2nd ed, Institute for Justice, 2015); Eric Blumenson and Eva Nilsen, 'Policing for Profit: The Drug War's Hidden Economic Agenda', *University of Chicago Law Review* (1998), 65(1): 35–114. Further concerns have been expressed as to 'potentially counter-productive aspects of the operation of ARIS': see HM Crown Prosecution Service Inspectorate, HM Inspectorate of Court Administration, and HM Inspectorate of Constabulary, *Joint Thematic Review of Asset Recovery: Restraint and Confiscation Casework* (Criminal Justice Joint Inspection, 2010), para. 6.1 *et seq*.

interest incompatible with his independent duties as a prosecutor' if the Director of the SFO were to opt for a resolution under POCA in preference to a fine.[113] Specifically in that case, as noted above, an agreement that had been agreed between the parties envisaged a settlement involving confiscation and civil recovery (both of which would fall under ARIS); that, however, was rejected by the court and instead a fine for the same amount was imposed (which was outside ARIS).[114] The 2014 change, taking the SFO out of ARIS, represents a better approach to the allocation of realised assets than does the incentivisation scheme. Not only does it provide certainty for the SFO itself (e.g. in terms of budget and resource planning), it also avoids criticism on grounds of conflict of interest and policing for profit.

In Scotland, ARIS does not apply. Indeed, it has been suggested that the excesses of 'policing for profit' have been avoided as a result: 'The absence of incentivisation has been instrumental in maintaining the focus of Part 5 recovery action in Scotland very firmly on the disruption of crime at all levels'.[115]

One innovative approach adopted in Scotland is the Cashback for Communities programme. According to its website,

CashBack for Communities is a Scottish Government programme which takes funds recovered from the proceeds of crime and invests them into free activities and programmes for young people across Scotland.[116]

Between 2008 and 2017, £92 million—recovered under POCA—was committed to the CashBack for Communities programme and other

---

[113] See *Innospec*, para. 36.

[114] *Innospec*, para. 47.

[115] Martin Collins and Colin King, 'The Disruption of Crime in Scotland Through Non-conviction Based Asset Forfeiture', *Journal of Money Laundering Control* (2003), 16(4): 379, 383.

[116] CashBack for Communities, Who We Are, available at: http://cashbackforcommunities.org/ (last accessed November 16, 2017). For further discussion of the use of realised assets under proceeds of crime legislation, see Barbara Vettori, 'The Disposal of Confiscated Assets in the EU Member States: What Works, What Does Not Work and What is Promising', in Colin King, Clive Walker, and Jimmy Gurulé (eds), *The Handbook of Criminal and Terrorism Financing Law* (Palgrave, 2018).

community initiatives.[117] Following the announcement of the Abbot Group CRO, for example, Justice Secretary Kenny MacAskill stated:

> This significant recovery made through the excellent work of the Civil Recovery Unit will be invested in the Scottish Government's hugely successful CashBack for Communities Programme which takes cash from the Proceeds of Crime and invests it in a range of sporting, cultural, community mentoring projects and sports facilities for the benefit of our young people and their communities. The £5.6m will be used to further expand the £46m CashBack Programme by funding projects that will contribute towards delivering youth employability, healthy lifestyles and reducing re-offending for the young people of Scotland.[118]

ENFORCEMENT LEGITIMACY AND TRANSPARENCY

Just because a CRO is conducted in an open and transparent manner does not necessarily render it legitimate.[119] But, the agreement of a CRO behind closed doors certainly raises concerns as to a lack of transparency. From April 2008 (when the SFO first obtained power to seek CROs[120]) up until July 2012 (when the SFO published details of the Oxford Publishing Ltd CRO), there was a noticeable lack of transparency surrounding CRO agreements entered into by the SFO. Change only came about following significant criticism. For example, in 2012 the lack of transparency was highlighted by the OECD as follows: 'A principal concern is the paucity of publicly available information on the foreign bribery cases conducted by the SFO that have been settled through civil

---

[117] CashBack for Communities, available at: http://cashbackforcommunities.org/ (last accessed November 16, 2017). For examples of such projects, see CashBack for Communities, *Annual Report 2015–2016* (Scottish Government, 2016). See also *National Evaluation of the CashBack for Communities Programme (April 2012–March 2014) Final Report* (ODS Consulting, 2014).

[118] Crown Office and Procurator Fiscal Services, *Press Release—Abbot Group Limited to Pay £5.6 million after Corruption Report* (November 23, 2012).

[119] See Donald R. Cressey, 'Negotiated Justice', *Criminology* (1968), 5(4): 5, 9.

[120] Serious Crime Act 2007 (Commencement No. 2 and Transitional and Transitory Provisions and Savings) Order 2008. Factors that might influence the use of non-conviction based powers are set out in Attorney General, *Guidance for prosecutors and investigators on their asset recovery powers under Section 2A of the Proceeds of Crime Act 2002* (November 29, 2012).

recovery orders'.[121] CROs facilitate behind-the-scenes negotiations/ agreements between the SFO and corporates with limited scrutiny:

> Unlike a criminal plea agreement, there is no court hearing. A Judge does not assess the factual basis of the order, or determine the amount that the defendant should pay. The judges and the SFO at the on-site visit described the procedure as "a paper process". The SFO and the defendant can thus dictate the terms of the settlement. Defendants therefore have the certainty in the outcome of settlement negotiations that is unavailable in the criminal plea negotiation process.[122]

A report from HM Crown Prosecution Service Inspectorate (HMCPSI) was also critical in this area, including one recommendation as follows: 'The SFO needs to design and document a transparent process for deciding to pursue civil recovery, and negotiating/agreeing any consent order'.[123] Indeed, the team preparing that HMCPSI report were not given access to earlier CRO cases:

> Civil recovery consent orders in cases settled before April 2012 are not disclosable, due to a provision in the orders themselves. Inspectors have not been allowed access to them, and we are therefore unable to comment on them.[124]

This reinforces the lack of transparency with such negotiations/ agreements.

Criticisms as to the lack of transparency surrounding CRO 'deals' in earlier cases has come from both proponents and critics. Some stakeholders have voiced concern that the use of such deals has allowed corporates and their directors 'to escape criminal justice on acceptance of a financial penalty'.[125] Often the SFO seemed at pains to avoid labelling

---

[121] OECD, *Phase 3 Report on Implementing the OECD Anti-Bribery Convention in the United Kingdom* (March 2012), p. 22.

[122] Ibid., p. 23. See also Transparency International (UK), *Deterring and Punishing Corporate Bribery: An Evaluation of UK Corporate Plea Agreements and Civil Recovery in Overseas Bribery Cases* (Transparency International, 2012), p. 64.

[123] HM Crown Prosecution Service Inspectorate (HMCPSI), *Report to the Attorney General on the inspection of the Serious Fraud Office* (November 2012), p. 3.

[124] Ibid., p. 35.

[125] Ibid.

the underlying conduct as 'criminal'.[126] Moreover, at least in earlier years there was no apparent basis as to how the monetary amounts were decided upon. Contrariwise, others have complained that the lack of transparency impacts on 'the negotiation process'—both for the SFO and corporates: 'the lack of a set, transparent process for handling self-referral makes the negotiation process harder to navigate for the SFO and those making the referral. Further, there are few accessible records of the negotiation and decision-making process'.[127]

A further point of criticism has been the lack of engagement with the case investigation teams. Often the case investigation teams found out about CRO agreements from staff at the corporate, rather than from other staff within the SFO. There was emphasis on 'the considerable risk that exclusion of the case team from the process, and inclusion of others who are less acquainted with the case, could lead to disadvantageous resolution'.[128]

Even before the HMCPSI report was published, the SFO did recognise the need for a transparent process in CRO cases, and published details of the OPL case in July 2012.[129] And, in 2017, during the next OECD evaluation (i.e. Phase 4), it was suggested that the SFO 'upholds an exemplary practice of publishing information about concluded foreign bribery cases on its website, which includes the date and location of offending, value of the bribe and the advantage received in return, and an explanation of how the penalties imposed were calculated'.[130] Yet, of the cases specifically mentioned by the OECD, only one—the OPL case—related to a CRO granted since the Phase 3 evaluation.[131] The extent to which the SFO merits plaudits for transparency in relation to CROs is debatable. Indeed, in 2014—as part of an HMCPSI follow-up

---

[126] Transparency International (UK), *Deterring and Punishing Corporate Bribery: An Evaluation of UK Corporate Plea Agreements and Civil Recovery in Overseas Bribery Cases* (Transparency International, 2012), pp. 63–64.

[127] HM Crown Prosecution Service Inspectorate (HMCPSI), *Report to the Attorney General on the Inspection of the Serious Fraud Office* (November 2012), p. 35.

[128] Ibid., p. 36.

[129] SFO Press Release, Oxford Publishing Ltd to Pay Almost £1.9 Million as Settlement After Admitting Unlawful Conduct in Its East African Operations (July 3, 2012).

[130] OECD, *Implementing the OECD Anti-Bribery Convention: Phase 4 Report: United Kingdom* (OECD, 2017), para. 156.

[131] The cases specifically cited in support were: Innospec; Smith & Ouzman; Standard Bank; XYZ Ltd; Oxford Publishing Ltd; Sweett Group; and Chapman (Securency).

inspection—the SFO was deemed to have 'made good progress in setting out the basis on which it will make decisions regarding alternative resolutions and civil recovery orders in particular',[132] however, it was also emphasised that there is still a lack of clarity as to the actual process.

In relation to Scotland, the OECD Phase 4 evaluation commented specifically on the Abbott Group and International Tubular Services cases:

> Those press releases provide limited information. The press release for Abbot Group identifies the date of the offending and name of the company, and asserts that the amount recovered (GBP 5.6m) represents the advantage received by the company. However, missing are details about the location of the offending, the bribe recipient and the subsidiary involved, the value of the bribe, and how the advantage was calculated. The International Tubular Services press release lacks similar information. Both press releases state that "In view of any criminal investigation of others that may follow, it is not possible to provide any further details of the corrupt payments", but there does not appear to have been any other enforcement activity taken in connection with these cases. The Working Group would expect Scotland to provide more comprehensive information about any foreign bribery cases concluded in future.[133]

That report recommended that Scotland should make public all relevant details of finalised cases. It was emphasised that 'transparency with respect to concluded cases is critical for deterrence and awareness, and to enable the Working Group to conduct a proper assessment of whether sanctions are effective, proportionate and dissuasive in practice'.[134]

---

[132] HM Crown Prosecution Service Inspectorate (HMCPSI), *Follow-up Inspection of the Serious Fraud Office* (November 2014), p. 31.

[133] OECD, *Implementing the OECD Anti-Bribery Convention: Phase 4 Report: United Kingdom* (OECD, 2017), para. 157.

[134] Ibid., p. 60.

CHAPTER 4

Deferred Prosecution Agreements: Law and Policy

Abstract This chapter examines the law and policy relating to the implementation of Deferred Prosecution Agreements. This chapter examines the legal framework and considers the advantages and disadvantages of DPAs.

Keywords Corporate crime · Deferred Prosecution Agreements · Crime and Courts Act 2013 · Code of Practice · HSBC

INTRODUCTION

This chapter analyses the law, policy and practice relating to the implementation of deferred prosecution agreements (DPAs). The DPA regime was brought into force in 2014[1] and provides law enforcement authorities, primarily the Serious Fraud Office (SFO) but also approved CPS prosecutors, with a (hybrid) criminal law mechanism for dealing with corporate crime. The DPA tool offers a 'third-way' to concluding

---

[1] Crime and Courts Act 2013, s.45 and Sched.17; Crime and Courts Act 2013 (Commencement No. 8) Order 2014. For detailed analysis of the framework, see Michael Bisgrove and Mark Weekes, 'Deferred Prosecution Agreements: A Practical Consideration', *Criminal Law Review* (2014), 6: 416; Polly Sprenger, *Deferred Prosecution Agreements: The Law and Practice of Negotiated Corporate Criminal Penalties* (Sweet and Maxwell, 2015).

© The Author(s) 2018
C. King and N. Lord, *Negotiated Justice and Corporate Crime*, Crime Prevention and Security Management,
https://doi.org/10.1007/978-3-319-78562-2_4

cases of corporate misconduct within the criminal law framework, as an alternative to civil recovery orders (CROs) (see Chapter 3) and to the pursuit of full criminal prosecution (see Chapter 6). In these terms, it represents a 'para-criminal' concept that needs to be scrutinised in line with concepts of legitimacy and justice.

This chapter analyses how DPAs enable enforcement authorities to circumvent pragmatic obstacles to the criminal prosecution of corporates, such as the restrictive requirements of the 'identification' principle. Moreover, DPAs also represent ideological and normative preferences of state actors for *negotiating* 'justice' in cases of serious corporate financial crimes. We first outline the legal basis and 'rules' of the DPA regime, analysing its key features and challenges. Second, we critically engage with arguments that the enforcement response to corporate crime is more 'effective' with the DPA regime. To do this we draw on case studies to provide concrete insights into how SFO policy translates into practice and to identify advantages and disadvantages with the regime, drawing attention to key emerging issues at this early stage of implementation. Third, we conceptualise the processes inherent in agreeing deferred prosecution (i.e. negotiation, cooperation, reformation) and the associated outcomes. In this we question whether 'justice' can really be achieved through DPAs, again with emphasis on the *legitimacy* of such a response. Alternatively, it is important to consider whether DPAs represent an extended 'accommodation' of corporate crimes by the state.

DPAs in the UK: A Brief Overview

In 2012, HM Government conceded that '[t]he present justice system in England and Wales is inadequate for dealing effectively with criminal enforcement against commercial organisations in the field of complex and serious economic crime'.[2] It was further stated that '[i]t is in the interests of justice and of economic well-being that investigators and prosecutors should be equipped with the right tools to tackle economic crime'.[3] Following a consultation on DPAs in 2013, the UK Government responded by recognising 'the pernicious and damaging

[2] Ministry of Justice, *Consultation on a New Enforcement Tool to Deal with Economic Crime Committed by Commercial Organisations: Deferred Prosecution Agreements* (Cm 8348) (May 2012), para. 23.

[3] Ibid., para. 22.

effect of corporate economic crime on our economy, and referred to the "general recognition" that options for dealing with offending by commercial organisations are currently limited and the number of outcomes each year, through both criminal and civil proceedings, is "too low"'.[4] The outcome of this was the introduction of DPAs, under the Crime and Courts Act 2013, as an additional response to the use of criminal prosecution and/or civil recovery, despite those remaining 'useful tools'.[5]

It is of note that an explicit justification for the need of such an enforcement mechanism by the Ministry of Justice was based on the perception that commercial organisations that could be prosecuted in England and Wales would instead choose to engage with US authorities, such as the Department of Justice (DOJ) and the Securities and Exchange Commission (SEC), where DPAs (and non-prosecution agreements (NPAs)) could be sought, in order to prevent action being taken in England and Wales.[6] It was argued that the 'lack of equivalent enforcement tools for UK prosecutors makes *negotiations* between UK and US prosecutors, and ultimately resolution of the case, difficult' (emphasis added).[7] The DPA Code of Practice in the UK includes a section on the process for invitation to enter into negotiations[8]; thus, the centrality of negotiation to responding to corporate financial crimes has been evident since the initial consultations and discussions on the implementation of DPAs.

In February 2014, DPAs became available to the Director of the SFO and approved CPS prosecutors. DPAs are not available in Scotland but the OECD has encouraged the Scottish system to come in line with England and Wales in order to overcome weaknesses in the current resolution of bribery cases through civil settlements

---

[4] Monty Raphael, *Bribery: Law and Practice* (Oxford University Press, 2016), p. 73.

[5] Ministry of Justice, *Consultation on a New Enforcement Tool to Deal with Economic Crime Committed by Commercial Organisations: Deferred Prosecution Agreements* (Cm 8348) (May 2012), para. 29. For consideration of the 'payoffs' and 'pitfalls' of using DPAs, see Simon Bronitt, 'Regulatory Bargaining in the Shadows of Preventive Justice: Deferred Prosecution Agreements', in Tamara Tulich, Rebecca Ananian-Welsh, Simon Bronitt, and Sarah Murray (eds), *Regulating Preventive Justice: Principle, Policy and Paradox* (Routledge, 2017).

[6] Ibid., para. 40. For further discussion of double jeopardy in this context, see Frederick T. Davis, 'International Double Jeopardy: U.S. Prosecutions and the Developing Law in Europe', *American University International Law Review* (2016), 31(1): 57.

[7] Ibid., para. 40.

[8] SFO/CPS, *Deferred Prosecution Agreements Code of Practice* (2013), p. 7.

and to ensure consistency across the UK response.[9] While DPAs were primarily introduced in response to foreign bribery cases, the legislation indicates a range of offences for which DPAs can be used. In addition to the offences of the Bribery Act 2010, these include the common law offences of conspiracy to defraud and cheating the public revenues, as well as specified statutory offences under the Theft Act 1968, the Customs and Excise Management Act 1979, the Forgery and Counterfeiting Act 1981, the Companies Act 1985, the Value Added Tax Act 1994, the Financial Services and Markets Act 2000, the Proceeds of Crime Act 2002, the Companies Act 2006, the Fraud Act 2006 and the Money Laundering Regulations 2017. Ancillary offences in relation to these provisions such as aiding, abetting, counselling or procuring the commission of the offence are also covered.[10]

What Is a DPA?

A DPA is a discretionary tool to be used by the prosecutor that enables a formal, voluntary agreement between a prosecutor and a corporate to be reached with judicial approval whereby a criminal prosecution for alleged criminal conduct can be deferred in exchange for the fulfilment of certain 'terms'. As Leveson P states, 'Its purpose is to provide a mechanism whereby an organisation (being a body corporate, a partnership or an unincorporated association, but not an individual) can avoid prosecution for certain economic or financial offences by entering into an agreement on negotiated terms with a prosecutor designated by the 2013 Act.'[11]

Possible terms of a DPA include, but are not limited to, a financial penalty; compensation to victims; donations to charities/third parties; disgorgement of any profits made; implementation of a rigorous internal compliance/training programme; cooperation in any investigation; and payment of reasonable costs to the prosecutor.[12] Other possible terms include prohibition from engaging in certain activities; financial

---

[9] OECD, *Implementing the OECD Anti-Bribery Convention. Phase 4 Report: United Kingdom* (OECD, 2017), p. 59.

[10] Crime and Courts Act 2013, Sched.17, Part 2: 'Offences in Relation to Which a DPA May Be Entered into'.

[11] *SFO v Standard Bank plc (now known as ICBC Standard Bank plc)*, Southwark Crown Court, Case No: U20150854, November 30, 2015, para. 1.

[12] Crime and Courts Act 2013, Sched.17, para. 5.

reporting obligations; robust monitoring; and cooperation with sector wide investigations.

In order to enter into a DPA the prosecutor must apply a two-stage test involving an evidential stage and a public interest stage. First, the prosecutor must be satisfied that the evidential stage of the Full Code Test in the Code for Crown Prosecutors is satisfied. If this is not met, the prosecutor must be satisfied that there is 'at least a reasonable suspicion based upon some admissible evidence' that the corporate has committed an offence, and that there are 'reasonable grounds for believing that a continued investigation would provide further admissible evidence within a reasonable period of time, so that all the evidence together would be capable of establishing a realistic prospect of conviction in accordance with the Full Code Test.'[13] Second, the prosecutor must be satisfied that the public interest would be properly served by entering into a DPA with the corporate.[14] If this two-stage test is passed and a DPA is considered appropriate, an indictment will be preferred (where the court approves the DPA) but will then be immediately suspended.[15] Where the two-stage test is not passed, and where it is not considered appropriate to continue the criminal investigation, the prosecutor should consider whether a civil recovery order is appropriate.[16]

Any agreement reached between the prosecutor and the corporate is subject to court approval[17] where it must be demonstrated at a preliminary and final hearing[18] that the agreement is in the 'interests

---

[13] SFO/CPS, *Deferred Prosecution Agreements Code of Practice* (2013), para. 1.2.i. The Code of Practice states that 'a reasonable time period will depend on all the facts and circumstances of the case, including its size, type and complexity' (para. 1.4).

[14] Ibid., para. 1.2.ii.

[15] Ibid., para. 1.5.

[16] Ibid., para. 1.6.

[17] For a critique of this judicial oversight, see Michael Bisgrove and Mark Weekes, 'Deferred Prosecution Agreements: A Practical Consideration', *Criminal Law Review* (2014), 6: 416, 428 *et seq.*

[18] Though there has been criticism about a lack of clarity as to the role of the court, and when prosecutors should first approach the court. For example, Grasso notes: 'the letter of the statute, pointing to the latest suitable moment in which the court can be approached, does not clarify when exactly prosecutors should first contact the court. In truth, as prosecutors must apply for a declaration on the suitability of already conceived and "proposed" terms, it seems that they could contact the court at quite an advanced phase of negotiations. Considered in those terms, this preliminary involvement seems to produce a sort of

of justice', and that the proposed terms are 'fair, reasonable and proportionate'.[19] Bronitt suggests that 'Judicial involvement in this process seeks to address the legitimacy deficit and mitigates the risk that a party may be unduly pressured by the prosecution to submit to the terms of an agreement that is not in the public interest, or is unfair, unreasonable or disproportionate.'[20] At the expiry of the DPA, unless the terms have been breached, proceedings will be discontinued. Alternatively, if these terms are not met, the prosecutor maintains the right to prosecute.

The DPA Code of Practice indicates that the SFO expects a high level of cooperation, honesty and proactive engagement from the corporate in order for a DPA to be suitable.[21] Engagement by the regulated community is important for legitimation of DPAs as an enforcement response. This engagement was expected to take the form of a 'self-report' to the enforcement authorities by the implicated corporate once they had become aware of a potential crime issue within their business though this would usually follow an internal investigation, sometimes involving external legal counsel.[22] While the first two DPAs negotiated by the SFO with Standard Bank and 'XYZ Ltd' (an anonymous SME) involved 'self-reports', this was not the case with Rolls Royce as the SFO became aware of the corruption via whistleblowers. This is an important issue, which will be discussed further later.

---

redundancy.' Costantino Grasso, 'Peaks and Troughs of the English Deferred Prosecution Agreement: The Lesson Learned from the DPA Between the SFO and ICBCSB Plc', *Journal of Business Law* (2014), 5: 388, 397.

[19] SFO/CPS, *Deferred Prosecution Agreements Code of Practice* (2013), paras. 9.4 and 10.3.

[20] Simon Bronitt, 'Regulatory Bargaining in the Shadows of Preventive Justice: Deferred Prosecution Agreements', in Tamara Tulich, Rebecca Ananian-Welsh, Simon Bronitt, and Sarah Murray (eds), *Regulating Preventive Justice: Principle, Policy and Paradox* (Routledge, 2017), p. 219.

[21] SFO/CPS, *Deferred Prosecution Agreements Code of Practice* (2013), paras. 2.8.2 and 2.9.1 *et seq.*

[22] For an overview of 'self-reporting' see Nicholas Lord, *Regulating Corporate Bribery in International Business: Anti-corruption in the UK and Germany* (Ashgate, 2014), pp. 120–124; Polly Sprenger, *Deferred Prosecution Agreements: The Law and Practice of Negotiated Corporate Criminal Penalties* (Sweet and Maxwell, 2015), ch. 10.

As part of the DPA the commercial organisation and prosecutor would also agree to a *negotiated* 'statement of facts', detailing the nature of the wrongdoing.[23] The Code explicitly states that the 'The parties should *resolve* any factual issues necessary to allow the court to agree terms of the DPA on a clear, fair and accurate basis'[24] (emphasis added). It continues: 'The court does not have the power to adjudicate upon factual differences in DPA proceedings.'[25] Similarly, the DPA consultation explicitly stated that the statement of facts would be *negotiated*.[26] How a 'statement of facts' can be resolved or negotiated is an interesting insight into the construction of social realities and we can gain insight into these processes by analysing cases involving DPAs. That said, to ensure the regulated community is 'on board' with the approach, such concessions over terminology may be necessary, particularly where there are concerns over stigma and labelling (though these may be useful in terms of crime reduction and calling corporates to answer for wrongdoing[27]).

Scrutinising DPAs: Some Advantages and Disadvantages

The decision to introduce DPAs to England and Wales was informed by their perceived 'success' in the US where they are widely used by the DOJ and SEC.[28] In the US, a 'turning point'[29] in the expanded use of DPAs was the prosecution and initial conviction of accountancy firm Arthur Andersen for obstructing justice in the Enron case. While there had been discussions as to the possibility of a DPA in

---

[23] SFO/CPS, *Deferred Prosecution Agreements Code of Practice* (2013), para. 6.

[24] Ibid., para. 6.2.

[25] Ibid.

[26] Ministry of Justice, *Consultation on a New Enforcement Tool to Deal with Economic Crime Committed by Commercial Organisations: Deferred Prosecution Agreements* (Cm 8348) (May 2012), para. 87.

[27] Such issues are explored in Chapter 6.

[28] It has been said that the use of DPAs acts as a means of restoring equilibrium in the prosecution of corporates. See Robert J. Ridge and Mackenzie A. Baird, 'The Pendulum Swings Back: Revisiting Corporate Criminality and the Rise of Deferred Prosecution Agreements', *University of Dayton Law Review* (2008), 33(2): 197; Peter Spivack and Sujit Raman, 'Regulating the 'New Regulators': Current Trends in Deferred Prosecution Agreements', *American Criminal Law Review* (2008), 45: 159.

[29] Brandon L. Garrett, 'Structural Reform Prosecution', *Virginia Law Review* (2007), 93: 853, 880.

that case, ultimately no DPA was agreed and a criminal prosecution was successfully brought (though the conviction was eventually overturned).[30] Arthur Andersen subsequently went out of business, which has led to the term 'Arthur Andersen Effect' being used in reference to corporates going out of business as a result of criminal conviction.[31] However, there have been concerns in the US about the use of DPAs. For example, there have been concerns that DPAs 'limit the punitive and deterrent value of the government's law enforcement efforts and extinguish the societal condemnation that should accompany criminal prosecution',[32] and that their use has increased the quantity of cases dealt with, but has lowered the quality of FCPA enforcement.[33] That is, '[i]nstances in which the DOJ brings actual criminal charges against a business organisation or otherwise insists in the resolution that the legal entity pleads guilty to FCPA violations represent a higher-quality FCPA enforcement action (in the eyes of the DOJ) and is thus more likely to result in related FCPA criminal charges against company employees'.[34] In contrast, where the result is a DPA or NPA that, according to Koehler, represents a 'lower-quality' enforcement action. Table 4.1 identifies several purported advantages and disadvantages of the use of DPAs.

[30] The conviction was overturned due to error in instructing the jury. *Arthur Andersen LLP v United States* 544 US 696 (2005) 374 F.3d 281, reversed and remanded. The government did not seek a retrial as the firm was no longer in business. Carrie Johnson, 'U.S. Ends Prosecution of Arthur Andersen', *Washington Post* (November 23, 2005).

[31] The Arthur Andersen case was specifically mentioned in the DPA Consultation: Ministry of Justice, *Consultation on a New Enforcement Tool to Deal with Economic Crime Committed by Commercial Organisations: Deferred Prosecution Agreements* (Cm 8348) (May 2012), para. 28. For further discussion of this case, see Elizabeth K. Ainslie, 'Indicting Corporations Revisited: Lessons of the Arthur Andersen Prosecution', *American Criminal Law Review* (2006), 43: 107. But see Gabriel Markoff, 'Arthur Andersen and the Myth of the Corporate Death Penalty: Corporate Criminal Convictions in the Twenty-First Century', *University of Pennsylvania Journal of Business Law* (2013), 15(3): 797, where it is argued that there is no evidence to support the 'Arthur Andersen Effect'.

[32] David M. Uhlmann, 'Deferred Prosecution and Non-prosecution Agreements and the Erosion of Corporate Criminal Liability', *Maryland Law Review* (2013), 72(4): 1302.

[33] Mike Koehler, 'Measuring the Impact of Non-prosecution and Deferred Prosecution Agreements on Foreign Corrupt Practices Act Enforcement', *University of California, Davis Law Review* (2015), 49: 497.

[34] Ibid., p. 544.

Table 4.1 Purported advantages and disadvantages of DPAs[a]

Advantages	Disadvantages
• An opportunity to restore equilibrium in the prosecution of corporates? • Enables a corporate to make full reparation for criminal behaviour without the collateral damage of a conviction i.e. the 'spill-over' effects • Concluded in the UK under the supervision of a judge, who must be convinced that the DPA is 'in the interests of justice' and that the terms are 'fair, reasonable and proportionate' • Avoids lengthy and costly trials, but allows transparency • Provides scope for a variety of large financial penalties such as reparation and compensation, where appropriate • Foregrounds structural and cultural reform	• Limits the punitive and deterrent value of the government's law enforcement efforts—i.e. 'out of court, out of mind' • Extinguishes the societal condemnation that should accompany criminal prosecution • Increases the quantity of cases dealt with but has lowered the quality of enforcement • Abuses of prosecutorial discretion due to a lack of judicial oversight (in US, not UK) • DPAs inconsistent with the rule of law • Does UK corporate criminal liability and sanction severity generate motivation to agree like in the US? • Hinders the development of case law and precedent • Overreliance on a company's internal investigations?

[a]Adapted from Nicholas Lord and Colin King, 'Negotiating Non-Contention: Civil Recovery and Deferred Prosecution in Response to Transnational Corporate Bribery', in Liz Campbell and Nicholas Lord (eds), *Corruption in Commercial Enterprise* (Routledge, 2018)

Critique in the US has indicated abuses of prosecutorial discretion due to a lack of judicial oversight,[35] raising concerns that prosecutors' use of DPAs is inconsistent with the rule of law.[36] Inconsistencies between the rule of law and enforcement responses create issues for legitimacy at a normative and legal level where the performance of the authorities deviates from the rules that have been established.[37] It has also been argued that '[a]lthough DPAs…may offer some short-term benefits, such as quicker resolution, long-term reliance on DPAs…as primary enforcement mechanisms in corporate law imposes significant costs, both to the market

---

[35] Robert J. Ridge and Mackenzie A. Baird, 'The Pendulum Swings Back: Revisiting Corporate Criminality and the Rise of Deferred Prosecution Agreements', *University of Dayton Law Review* (2008), 33(2): 197, 203.

[36] Jennifer Arlen, 'Prosecuting Beyond the Rule of Law: Corporate Mandates Imposed Through Deferred Proseuction Agreements', *Journal of Legal Analysis* (2016), 8(1): 191.

[37] See David Beetham, *The Legitimation of Power* (2nd ed, Palgrave Macmillan, 2013).

and federal law'.[38] For example, DPAs hinder the development of case law and precedent that are used to establish the boundaries of permissible behaviour; this in turn creates regulatory uncertainties that can increase the costs to corporates investing abroad as they attempt to determine efficient and optimal legal frameworks (i.e. what is legally permissible).[39]

Notwithstanding these criticisms, it is recognised that notable differences exist in the system in England and Wales, such as the requirement of early judicial oversight and court approval.[40] However, a core theory failure in the policy transfer to England and Wales was the failure to acknowledge difficulties of corporate criminal liability (in the UK),[41] in particular the reality that prosecution is rare.[42] Moreover, the severity of sanctions in the US generates a motivation (in the US) to agree to a DPA that is largely lacking in England and Wales. There are issues in terms of legitimacy here as some UK corporates have preferred to agree sanctions in the US for this reason,[43]

---

[38] Allen R. Brooks, 'A Corporate Catch-22: How Deferred and Non-prosecution Agreements Impede the Full Development of the Foreign Corrupt Practices Act', *Journal of Law, Economics and Policy* (2010), 7: 155.

[39] Ibid., p. 156.

[40] SFO/CPS, *Deferred Prosecution Agreements Code of Practice* (2013), para. 9 ('preliminary hearing(s)') and 10 ('application for approval'). See Michael Bisgrove and Mark Weekes, 'Deferred Prosecution Agreements: A Practical Consideration', *Criminal Law Review* (2014), 6: 416, 428 *et seq* for consideration of judicial oversight.

[41] It must be acknowledged, though, that such difficulties are now mitigated somewhat by 'failure' offences, such as failure to prevent bribery and failure to prevent the criminal facilitation of tax evasion. These offences are contained in the Bribery Act 2010 and the Criminal Finances Act 2017, respectively. Failure offences involve a form of strict liability that circumvents the need to 'identify' the guilt of the controlling minds of the company.

[42] This is particularly true for larger corporates. This issue is discussed further in Chapter 6.

[43] This concern was explicitly emphasised in the DPA consultation: 'Commercial organisations which could be prosecuted in both England and Wales and the US may choose to engage with US authorities so as to prevent action being taken in England and Wales. Resolving a case in the US may also be attractive given the wider and more flexible range of enforcement tools, including non-prosecution agreements (NPAs) and DPAs which do not result in a criminal conviction. The lack of equivalent enforcement tools for UK prosecutors makes negotiations between UK and US prosecutors, and ultimately resolution of the case, difficult.' Ministry of Justice, *Consultation on a New Enforcement Tool to Deal with Economic Crime Committed by Commercial Organisations: Deferred Prosecution Agreements* (Cm 8348) (May 2012), para. 40.

perhaps indicating a greater level of shared values and beliefs between large corporates and the US DPA system.

In England and Wales, there is no requirement for formal admissions of guilt—though corporates must 'admit the contents and meaning of key documents referred to in the statement of facts'.[44] As Sprenger notes, 'The statement of facts is not necessarily an admission of guilt of the offence, but rather acceptance of the existence of facts the prosecutor alleges would constitute the elements of the offences charged.'[45] The reader may ask themselves why it is that a corporate would agree to the terms of a DPA (e.g. substantial fine, monitoring) to settle a case if it is not admitting to any wrongdoing. Cynically, it might be argued that corporates may prefer the route of a DPA as, with no formal admissions of guilt, the corporate will be less liable to class actions (e.g. from disgruntled shareholders or investors) and lateral litigation (e.g. from competitors). Furthermore, closure and certainty (key for audience legitimacy) will be provided following the completion of the DPA. There is also anecdotal evidence that share prices of companies agreeing DPAs increase following public notification.[46] The SFO Director David Green suggested other benefits of DPAs are that they avoid a prosecution and the stigma of a possible conviction, they can be in private until the final declaration, they speed up the investigative process and save on the costs and paralysis attendant on a full criminal investigation, they permit at least some influence and control by the corporate, they improve the company's culture of compliance and prevention and they may avoid disqualification from tendering for EU public contracts following a conviction.[47] Furthermore, it might also be argued that DPAs reflect normative preferences for the principal role of corporate criminal enforcement to be about the structural reform

---

[44] SFO/CPS, *Deferred Prosecution Agreements Code of Practice* (2013), para. 6.3.

[45] Polly Sprenger, *Deferred Prosecution Agreements: The Law and Practice of Negotiated Corporate Criminal Penalties* (Sweet and Maxwell, 2015), p. 333.

[46] Peggy Hollinger and Catherine Belton, 'Rolls-Royce Shares Climb on Back of Bribery Settlement', *Financial Times* (January 17, 2017).

[47] David Green, 'Ethical Business Conduct: An Enforcement Perspective' Speech at *PricewaterhouseCoopers* (March 6, 2014).

of corrupt corporate cultures rather than indictment, prosecution and punishment.[48]

At the same time as DPAs have been introduced in England and Wales, 'there is increasing scrutiny of these agreements in the US and a larger debate about the appropriate use of such enforcement tools by regulators'.[49] The inclination to resort to DPAs reflects prosecutors' willingness to compromise when corporates are 'too big to jail'.[50] Thus, the fledgling use of DPAs in the UK coincides with increased scrutiny and criticism in the US.

This point raises an important political-economic consideration. For instance, in December 2017 a DPA between US authorities and UK bank HSBC expired.[51] This DPA arose from allegations that HSBC was in breach of anti-money laundering regulations, specifically in relation to the laundering of hundreds of millions of dollars belonging to Mexican and Columbian organised crime groups. The bank had also allegedly been handling financial transactions for actors in countries under US sanctions, including Iran, Libya, Sudan, Burma and Cuba.[52] Had the terms of the DPA been breached,[53] or full prosecution been completed, the

---

[48] Peter Spivack and Sujit Raman, 'Regulating the 'New Regulators': Current Trends in Deferred Proseuction Agreements', *American Criminal Law Review* (2008), 45: 159, 161.

[49] Monty Raphael, *Bribery: Law and Practice* (Oxford University Press, 2016), p. 166.

[50] See Jennifer Arlen, 'Prosecuting Beyond the Rule of Law: Corporate Mandates Imposed Through Deferred Proseuction Agreements', *Journal of Legal Analysis* (2016), 8(1): 191; Brandon Garrett, *Too Big To Jail: How Prosecutors Compromise with Corporations* (Harvard University Press, 2014).

[51] The DPA is available on the SEC website: https://www.sec.gov/Archives/edgar/data/83246/000119312512499980/d453978dex101.htm (last accessed January 12, 2018). See also Stephen Morris, 'HSBC Escapes Prosecution as U.S. Ends 5-Year Deferred Deal', *Bloomberg* (December 11, 2017).

[52] The 'Statement of Facts' is available on the DOJ website: https://www.justice.gov/sites/default/files/opa/legacy/2012/12/11/dpa-attachment-a.pdf (last accessed January 15, 2018). See also Jill Treanor and Dominic Rushe, 'HSBC Pays Record $1.9bn Fine to Settle US Money-Laundering Accusations', *The Guardian* (December 11, 2012).

[53] Indeed there have been various reports where concern was expressed as to HSBC's compliance with the terms of the DPA. See, for example, Scott McCulloch, HSBC'S Anti-Money Laundering Compliance Under Investigation (February 21, 2017), available at: https://www.insider.co.uk/news/hsbcs-anti-money-laundering-compliance-9896293 (last accessed January 15, 2018); Zacks Equity Research, DOJ to Rescind HSBC's Deferred-Prosecution Agreement? available at: http://www.nasdaq.com/article/doj-to-rescind-hsbcs-deferred-prosecution-agreement-cm676170 (last accessed January 15, 2018).

US government would no longer have been able to enter into business arrangements with the bank and HSBC's ability to conduct business in the US would have been at risk as its charter may have been revoked. Such an outcome would, of course, have had notable economic collateral damage for one of the UK's leading, global corporates (as well as for the UK itself).

It subsequently came to light that the then Chancellor of the Exchequer, George Osborne, and the then Financial Services Authority (FSA) intervened with US authorities. In a letter to the Chairman of the Federal Reserve, Osborne warned of jeopardising financial stability which could 'lead to contagion' and noted that '[q]uestions about HSBC's continued ability to clear US dollars would risk destabilising the bank globally, with very serious implications for financial and economic stability, particularly in Europe and Asia'.[54] As for the FSA, during an interagency coordination call:

> The FSA participants weighed in very strongly that any guilty plea would need to be carefully planned and coordinated, with all agencies having contingency plans in place in advance. They emphasized their view that HSBC is the second most systemically important bank in the world with substantial dollar holdings in the U.S. and overseas, and said that even the threat of a charter revocation could result in a global financial disaster. While the FSA folks did not argue specifically against a prosecution, it was clear they were very concerned about the reverberations such an action could have within the financial system, and they asked for urgent high level discussions with DOJ on the matter.[55]

Despite an internal recommendation to prosecute,[56] the DOJ leadership ultimately decided not to pursue criminal prosecution apparently due to concerns about collateral consequences both for the bank and

---

[54] 'Letter from Chancellor Osborne to Chairman Bernanke and Secretary Geithner (September 10, 2012)', in Jeb Hensarling (Chair), *Too Big to Jail: Inside The Obama Justice Department's Decision Not to Hold Wall Street Accountable*. Report Prepared by the Republican Staff of the Committee on Financial Services, U.S. House of Representatives (2016), available at: https://financialservices.house.gov/uploadedfiles/07072016_oi_tbtj_sr.pdf (last accessed January 12, 2018), Appendix 4.

[55] Ibid., p. 15.

[56] This recommendation was made by the DOJ Asset Forfeiture and Money Laundering Section. Ibid., p. 12.

the financial system.[57] The Hensarling report suggested that 'the FSA's intervention ... appears to have played a significant role in ultimately persuading DOJ not to prosecute HSBC.'[58]

Statements from US Treasury officials also indicated that there were concerns that the 'UK FSA was being particularly problematic on enforcement and adopting a light touch approach at industry's request'.[59] These interactions provide insights into the inevitably politically embedded nature of prosecuting major global corporates as well as the close relationships of industry, the executive and regulators in the UK. This poses important questions about the underlying transparency of decisions to pursue DPAs rather than full prosecution, as well as feeding concerns as to social fairness/justice. Inevitably, DPAs like in the HSBC case—and the process of their agreement—can widen the legitimacy deficit.

Furthermore, whilst the DPA for this particular money laundering case expired with no breach of the terms, two points are of interest to note. First, within the five year time-period of the DPA, HSBC has been further sanctioned in the US for failures to prevent the manipulation of the Foreign Exchange (Forex) currency markets,[60] reached an agreement[61] with authorities in France in November 2017 in relation to facilitating tax evasion,[62] and has been accused of 'possible criminal complicity' in the laundering of illicit finances from political corruption involving the Gupta family in South Africa.[63] Second, in January 2018 HSBC agreed another DPA in the US to resolve charges that it engaged in a scheme to defraud two bank clients through a multi-million dollar scheme commonly

[57] Ibid., p. 18.

[58] Ibid., p. 26.

[59] Ibid.

[60] Patrick Rucker, 'U.S. Fines HSBC $175 Million for Lax Forex Trading Oversight', *Reuters* (September 29, 2017).

[61] A Judicial Agreement in the Public Interest, which is modelled on DPAs in the US and UK. The French term for the agreement is Convention Judiciaire d'Intérêt Public (CJIP), under the Sapin II Law.

[62] David Keohane and Martin Arnold, 'HSBC Agrees to Pay €300m to Settle Probe into Tax Evasion', *Financial Times* (November 14, 2017).

[63] Rob Davies, 'HSBC "Complicit" in South Africa Scandal, House of Lords Told', *The Guardian* (November 1, 2017).

referred to as 'front-running'.[64] This latest DPA required HSBC to pay a \$63.1 million criminal penalty and \$38.4 million in disgorgement and restitution. Thus, while HSBC can claim to have 'lived up to all of its commitments' in relation to the US money laundering DPA, its claim to be 'able to combat financial crime much more effectively today as the result of the significant reforms we have implemented over the last five years'[65] is not entirely persuasive given its global activities. This case inevitably leads one to question the 'effectiveness'[66] of DPAs,[67] particularly in the context of global corporates and the limits of sovereign enforcement responses.

While there are clear political and ideological components to the use of DPAs, there are practical concerns over the use of DPAs in England and Wales. For instance, in the US, where DPAs have been deemed a 'success', the principle of vicarious liability applies. With vicarious liability a corporate can be held criminally liable for the acts or omissions of its individual employees as the criminal intent, and the performance of the legally prohibited act, are automatically attributed to the corporate.[68] In contrast, establishing whether a corporate can be criminally liable for the acts or omissions of individual employees in the UK is much more difficult, for example due to issues related to 'the corporate mind' and the 'identification principle'.[69] In other words, corporates

[64] Department of Justice, Press Release—HSBC Holdings Plc Agrees to Pay More Than \$100 Million to Resolve Fraud Charges (January 18, 2018).

[65] HSBC, 'News Release—HSBC Holdings Plc Expiration of 2012 Deferred Prosecution Agreement' (December 11, 2017), available at: http://www.hsbc.com/news-and-insight/media-resources/media-releases/2017/hsbc-holdings-plc-expiration-of-2012-deferred-prosecution-agreement (last accessed January 12, 2018).

[66] It is recognised that there are difficulties in measuring 'effectiveness' of law and enforcement responses. See, for example, Anthony Allott, 'The Effectiveness of Law', *Valparaiso University Law Review* (1981), 15: 229. For a multi-faceted definition of legal effectiveness, see W. Bradnee Chambers, 'Towards an Improved Understanding of Legal Effectiveness of International Environmental Treaties', *Georgetown International Environmental Law Review* (2004), 16: 501.

[67] See, generally, US Government Accountability Office, *Corporate Crime: DOJ Has Taken Steps to Better Track Its Use of Deferred and Non-Prosecution Agreements, but Should Evaluate Effectiveness.* GAO-10-110 (December 2009).

[68] Ved P. Nanda, 'Corporate Criminal Liability in the United States: Is a New Approach Warranted?' in Mark Pieth and Radha Ivory (eds), *Corporate Criminal Liability. Emergence, Convergence and Risk* (Springer, 2011), p. 65.

[69] See Chapter 6.

have been, and are more likely to be, prosecuted and convicted in the US which makes DPAs a credible and legitimate alternative. Thus, as mentioned earlier, there is a clear issue of policy transfer across jurisdictions here. Decisive in the success and impact of such transfers are the cultural, socio-political and institutional contexts at the receiving end.[70] The absence of a credible threat of corporate prosecution in the UK potentially undermines the tool. Notwithstanding, DPAs *have* been agreed with corporates in England and Wales. From the perspective of corporates a DPA can bring many benefits, including giving clarity and certainty by drawing a line under criminal behaviour and previous criminal conduct. The real test of the regime will emerge when a corporate rejects a DPA to contest a prosecution or when the terms of a DPA are breached, as prosecution should follow.

The Director of the SFO, David Green, has also indicated that DPAs avoid 'severe collateral damage to those (like employees, shareholders or pensioners) who had no part in the criminality prosecuted' and the route to a DPA will 'also be cheaper, quicker and more certain for all parties'.[71] There are some concerns here, however. The SFO must be wary of replacing the principles of the rule of law and criminal justice with what is cheap or quick. Furthermore, the issue of corporate criminal liability implies that small and medium enterprises are more likely to be criminally convicted; it is more straightforward to establish that the 'controlling mind' knew of offending behaviour in smaller organisations. This may result in the differential sanctioning of large and small business which raises questions of equality, and therefore legitimacy, before the law, as larger organisations will be better positioned to negotiate DPAs or civil settlements. A final point to mention here is that increased cooperation between large corporates and the state may have 'unintended' or 'collateral' consequences, such as the turning of corporates into agents of the state (i.e. self investigation and provision of evidence) with resulting corporate governance and constitutional implications.[72]

---

[70] Suzanne Karstedt, 'Creating Institutions: Linking the 'Local' and the 'Global' in the Travel of Crime Policies', *Police Practice and Research* (2007), 8(2): 145.

[71] David Green, 'Ethical Business Conduct: An Enforcement Perspective', Speech at *PricewaterhouseCoopers* (March 6, 2014).

[72] Barry A. Bohrer and Barbara L. Trencher, 'Prosecution Deferred: Exploring the Unintended Consequences and Future of Corporate Cooperation', *American Criminal Law Review* (2007), 44: 1481.

CHAPTER 5

Deferred Prosecution Agreements: In Practice

Abstract This chapter explores the use of Deferred Prosecution Agreements in practice, analysing the four DPAs that have been negotiated to date.

Keywords Corporate crime · Deferred Prosecution Agreements · Standard Bank DPA · XYZ Ltd DPA · Rolls Royce DPA · Tesco DPA · Public interest · Fair, reasonable and proportionate terms · Sentencing discount

At the time of writing, deferred prosecution agreements have been agreed and approved for three corporates implicated in transnational bribery (namely, Standard Bank, an anonymous SME and Rolls Royce) and one company involved in accountancy irregularities (namely, Tesco). Table 2.2 in Chapter 2 outlines the key features of these cases; here we explore each case in further detail in chronological order. Common features of all the DPAs include financial penalties such as standalone financial orders, disgorgement of profits (essentially a blend of a confiscation order and a recovery order), payment of prosecution costs and, in the case of Standard Bank, the payment of compensation. All cases also involve a requirement of cooperation and the implementation of improved compliance procedures so as to secure the maintenance of anti-bribery and anti-fraud standards.

© The Author(s) 2018
C. King and N. Lord, *Negotiated Justice and Corporate Crime*, Crime Prevention and Security Management, https://doi.org/10.1007/978-3-319-78562-2_5

83

Case 1—Standard Bank

In November 2015 the SFO negotiated the first DPA with Standard Bank, a UK regulated financial institution.[1] The case concerned a corrupt payment in March 2013 by a former sister company of Standard Bank, Stanbic Bank Tanzania, to a local partner in an attempt to secure a contract from the government of Tanzania. The case came to the attention of the SFO following a self-report by Standard Bank's solicitors, Jones Day, in April 2013. The time between the illicit payment and the report to the authorities was therefore relatively swift (particularly in comparison to other cases where the time between the offence(s), internal detection and external notification to the authorities can take years, rather than weeks).[2] This perhaps reflects the relatively straightforward nature of the case, in that only one suspicious payment was made, rather than a series of payments over time, and the case was a 'failure' offence[3] as opposed to a substantive active or passive bribery offence. Jones Day (solicitors acting for the bank) was instructed to investigate the payment and disclose findings to the SFO; this report was disclosed in July 2014. The report included evidence from email servers, inboxes and hard drives, electronic documents from shared drives and from others within the company, as well as paper files, CCTV footage from Africa and telephone recordings. The materials were reviewed by the SFO followed by its own interviews with those implicated and UK based employees involved in the transaction. Ultimately, the SFO Director, David Green, decided that the public interest would be met by a DPA. Negotiations were then started and the Agreement was approved by Lord Justice Leveson.

---

[1] SFO, 'Press Release—SFO Agrees First UK DPA with Standard Bank' (November 30, 2015); *SFO v Standard Bank plc (now known as ICBC Standard Bank plc)*, Southwark Crown Court, Case No: U20150854, November 30, 2015. For further discussion of this DPA, see Costantino Grasso, 'Peaks and Troughs of the English Deferred Prosecution Agreement: The Lesson Learned from the DPA Between the SFO and ICBCSB Plc', *Journal of Business Law* (2014), 5: 388.

[2] See Polly Sprenger, *Deferred Prosecution Agreements: The Law and Practice of Negotiated Corporate Criminal Penalties* (Sweet and Maxwell, 2015), ch. 9 for discussion of internal investigations (described as 'a matter of critical importance', p. 281), the first alert (i.e. 'the first point at which a corporation's management become aware of the allegations forming the basis of the misconduct', p. 282) and the timeliness of self-reporting.

[3] Bribery Act 2010, s. 7.

The DPA related to a failure to prevent bribery by Stanbic Bank Tanzania in contravention of Section 7 of the Bribery Act 2010. Following the approval of the DPA, the indictment was immediately suspended. The DPA terms involved compensation of US$6 million plus interest of US$1,046,196.58; disgorgement of profit of US$8.4 million; payment of a financial penalty of US$16.8 million; and payment of costs incurred by the SFO (£330,000).[4] It was also explicitly made clear that no tax reduction would be sought in relation to these payments. Furthermore, Standard Bank agreed to full and continued cooperation with the SFO and agreed to commission an independent review by PricewaterhouseCoopers LLP of its anti-bribery compliance procedures, with any recommendations to be implemented.[5]

Key Issues in the Standard Bank Case

It has been said by the SFO Director that the Standard Bank DPA was a 'landmark' agreement and would 'serve as a template for future agreements'.[6] It has also been suggested that '[t]his was a pre-packed, model case for both the SFO and the court to demonstrate the effectiveness not only of the recently introduced DPA legislation, but also of s7 of the Bribery Act itself'.[7] What then can we learn from this case?

First, there are questions about when DPAs are in the public interest. According to the Code of Practice,

Public interest factors that can affect the decision to prosecute usually depend on the seriousness of the offence, which includes the culpability of P and the harm to the victim. A prosecution will usually take place unless there are public interest factors against prosecution which outweigh those tending in favour of prosecution.[8]

---

[4] The exchange rate on the day in question was US1 = £0.6646439742.

[5] *SFO v Standard Bank plc (now known as ICBC Standard Bank plc)*, Southwark Crown Court, Case No: U20150854, November 30, 2015, paras. 12–13.

[6] SFO, 'Press Release—SFO Agrees First UK DPA with Standard Bank' (November 30, 2015).

[7] Edward Clough, 'First UK Deferred Prosecution Agreement Between the SFO and a Bank', *Allen and Overy, Litigation and Dispute Resolution Review* (April 2016), p. 21.

[8] SFO/CPS, *Deferred Prosecution Agreements Code of Practice* (2013), para. 2.5.

As the Standard Bank case concerned a 'failure' offence rather than a substantive bribery offence, it might be suggested (as Leveson P implied[9]) that it was less serious, particularly as it did not involve direct criminal culpability. Perhaps more importantly, Standard Bank responded swiftly to the payment, with early engagement with the SFO and extensive and frank cooperation. Indeed, Leveson P emphasised: 'Of particular significance was the promptness of the self-report, the fully disclosed internal investigation and cooperation of Standard Bank. Finally, also relevant were the agreement for an independent review of anti-corruption policies and the fact that Standard Bank is now differently owned, a majority shareholding having been acquired by ICBC'.[10] Given that this case was described as a 'template' by the SFO Director, it might be expected that swift self-reporting, self-investigation and extensive cooperation would be key factors in deciding to enter into DPA negotiations in future cases. (But contrast the Rolls Royce DPA, discussed later on.)

It is not known whether the proactive response of Standard Bank reflects an ethical and socially responsible corporate leadership, or an amoral calculation for the benefit of the business. For instance, had the case been much more complex with more extensive culpability, a more rational response may have been not to disclose the payment given the low risks of detection (and subsequent prosecution *if* detected at a later time) and uncertainty over the DPA process. Relatedly, it is important to note that this case was relatively straightforward—involving a single transaction that fell within the ambit of section 7 of the Bribery Act (i.e. a 'failure' offence), which perhaps enabled the corporate to self-report within a short time. Commenting on this case, Gallagher opines:

> Where the wrongdoing is more complex or the probability of successful prosecution more difficult to assess, it is likely that any self-report would be made significantly later (if at all). Whether the SFO would consider this as full cooperation, and a factor tending towards disposal via a DPA, remains to be seen.[11]

---

[9] *SFO v Standard Bank plc (now known as ICBC Standard Bank plc)*, Southwark Crown Court, Case No: U20150854, November 30, 2015, para. 14.

[10] Ibid.

[11] Ellen Gallagher, 'The Standard Bank DPA—The First of Many?', *International Bar Association Blog*, June 9, 2016, available at: https://www.ibanet.org/Article/Detail.aspx?ArticleUid=70d2382a-e94e-4d81-a12c-3bef0730747b (last accessed January 18, 2018).

Such a situation arose in the third UK DPA (Rolls Royce), discussed below.

A second, briefer, point relates to the terms of the Agreement. Leveson P was satisfied that the terms were 'fair, reasonable and proportionate'[12] (as is required for the Agreement to be approved). Significantly the legislation requires that 'The amount of any financial penalty agreed between the prosecutor and P must be broadly comparable to the fine that a court would have imposed on P on conviction for the alleged offence following a guilty plea'.[13] Taking account of Sentencing Council Guidelines,[14] Leveson P concluded that the appropriate penalty would be 300% of the total fee which would be reduced by one-third to reflect the earliest admission of responsibility.[15] There have been concerns, then, that this approach might not incentivise corporates to self-report with the aim of agreeing a DPA. For example, Gallagher states:

> given the fact that the financial penalty imposed pursuant to a DPA will be in line with that which would have been imposed upon conviction following an early guilty plea, it is difficult to see what most corporates would have to gain from self-reporting at all rather than waiting for the prosecution to present its case before considering what, if any, admissions it should make.[16]

We return to this issue in discussing the next DPA (XYZ Ltd), where the discount was increased to 50%.

---

[12] *SFO v Standard Bank plc (now known as ICBC Standard Bank plc)*, Southwark Crown Court, Case No: U20150854, November 30, 2015, para. 19.

[13] Crime and Courts Act 2013, Sched.17, para. 5(4).

[14] Sentencing Council, *Fraud, Bribery and Money Laundering Offences: Definitive Guideline* (2014). For further discussion of financial penalties in the UK, see Polly Sprenger, *Deferred Prosecution Agreements: The Law and Practice of Negotiated Corporate Criminal Penalties* (Sweet and Maxwell, 2015), p. 420 *et seq*.

[15] *SFO v Standard Bank plc (now known as ICBC Standard Bank plc)*, Southwark Crown Court, Case No: U20150854, November 30, 2015, para. 16. The financial penalty is considered in more detail at paras. 43–58 of the preliminary judgment (delivered on the same date as the judgment approving the Agreement).

[16] Ellen Gallagher, 'The Standard Bank DPA—The First of Many?', *International Bar Association Blog* (June 9, 2016).

Third, even though a corporate might enter into a DPA in the UK (with associated financial penalties, disgorgement, etc.) there remains the possibility that that corporate might also be pursued by law enforcement agencies in other jurisdictions. The main concern relates to the United States and potential for enforcement action to be taken there, as the fact that a DPA has been entered into in the UK would not be a bar to such action; in other words double jeopardy would not apply in the US.[17] It has been said that '[t]his lack of certainty about treatment elsewhere is a significant disincentive to any company considering signing up to a DPA'.[18] As Davis argues, in the context of the OECD Anti-Bribery Convention,

> The adamant refusal of U.S. prosecuting authorities and courts to recognize any limits on their power to engage in prosecutions that duplicate prosecutions abroad, coupled with the near-total silence of the Department of Justice on the standards it will apply to respect negotiated outcomes in other countries by declining prosecution, does a disservice to the goal of the OECD Convention, and to the goal of coordinated prosecutions generally, because it creates a disincentive to other countries to adopt flexible outcomes such as a DPA, and to companies that might otherwise elect to enter into discussions with authorities in their "home" country or in a country with a substantial interest in the matter.[19]

In the Standard Bank DPA, it is significant that this lack of certainty was addressed at an early stage: authorities in both Tanzania and the US were informed of the proposed UK DPA. Tanzanian authorities opened its own investigation into Stanbic. They did not object to the UK DPA.[20] In the US, the DOJ indicated that it would drop its own investigation if

---

[17] Frederick T. Davis, 'International Double Jeopardy: U.S. Prosecutions and the Developing Law in Europe', *American University International Law Review* (2016), 31(1): 57.

[18] Edward Clough, 'First UK Deferred Prosecution Agreement Between the SFO and a Bank', *Allen and Overy, Litigation and Dispute Resolution Review* (April 2016), p. 22.

[19] Frederick T. Davis, 'International Double Jeopardy: U.S. Prosecutions and the Developing Law in Europe', *American University International Law Review* (2016), 31(1): 57, 100.

[20] *SFO v Standard Bank plc (now known as ICBC Standard Bank plc)*, Southwark Crown Court, Case No: U20150854, November 30, 2015, para. 18.

the matter is resolved in the UK,[21] and the SEC concluded its own investigations and—aware of the proposed UK DPA—accepted a civil money penalty of $4.2 million on the same day.[22] That notwithstanding, there remain potential issues with such an informal, and ad hoc, approach including 'the possible violation of the principle of foreseeability, legal certainty and protection of legitimate expectations that may lead to unfair decisions and preferential treatments for certain corporations'.[23]

A final consideration—which has arisen subsequent to the approval of the DPA—relates to when fresh proceedings can be commenced against a corporate. The Code of Practice states: 'If P provides inaccurate, misleading or incomplete information where P knew or ought to have known that the information was inaccurate, misleading or incomplete, the prosecutor may instigate fresh proceedings against P for the same alleged offence in accordance with paragraph 11 of Schedule 17 to the Act notwithstanding any DPA that may have been approved'.[24] Paragraph 11 of Schedule 17 provides that 'Where proceedings are discontinued under sub-paragraph (1), fresh criminal proceedings may not be instituted against P for the alleged offence'.[25] This prohibition does not apply, however, where the corporate provided inaccurate, misleading or incomplete information and ought to have known that the information was inaccurate, misleading or incomplete.[26] There have been allegations that Standard Bank misrepresented facts in negotiating the DPA.[27] It remains to be seen what, if any, effect this might have.

---

[21] *SFO v Standard Bank plc (now known as ICBC Standard Bank plc), Preliminary DPA Judgment*, Southwark Crown Court, Case No: U20150854, November 30, 2015, para. 58.
[22] SEC, 'Press Release—Standard Bank to Pay $4.2 Million to Settle SEC Charges' (November 30, 2015).
[23] Costantino Grasso, 'Peaks and Troughs of the English Deferred Prosecution Agreement: The Lesson Learned from the DPA Between the SFO and ICBCSB Plc', *Journal of Business Law* (2014), 5: 388, 407.
[24] SFO/CPS, *Deferred Prosecution Agreements Code of Practice* (2013), para. 4.3.
[25] Crime and Courts Act 2013, Sched.17, para. 11(2).
[26] Ibid., para. 11(3).
[27] David Connett, 'Tanzanians Slam SFO's Plea Bargain on African Corruption Case', *Independent* (March 15, 2016); Moyagabo Maake, 'Standard Sued by Former Tanzanian Official Ensnared in Bribery Scandal', *Business Live* (May 20, 2016).

Case 2—'XYZ Ltd'

In July 2016 the SFO's second DPA was approved, again by Lord Justice Leveson. The company in this case was an anonymous UK SME, referred to only as 'XYZ Ltd' due to on-going and related legal proceedings. The SME's employees and agents were involved in the systematic offer and/or payment of bribes to secure contracts to supply its products in foreign jurisdictions between June 2004 and June 2012. The bribery came to attention after XYZ's parent company 'ABC' in the US implemented a global compliance programme in 2011 which resulted in concerns raised with XYZ in 2012. XYZ responded by having an independent law firm undertake an internal investigation. This investigation involved analysing over 90 GB of electronic data from the company server, laptop hard drives and external memory drives, reviewing over 27,000 electronic records and hard copy documents, as well as conducting 13 interviews with four XYZ employees. The firm self-reported to the SFO formally, following an earlier meeting, in January 2013.

The indictment related to conspiracy to corrupt and conspiracy to bribe,[28] and failure to prevent bribery.[29] This indictment was suspended following approval of the DPA. The DPA involved financial orders of £6,553,085, comprised of a £6,201,085 disgorgement of gross profits and a £352,000 financial penalty. (The SFO agreed not to seek costs.) Here too it was explicitly made clear that no tax reduction would be sought in relation to these payments. The company also agreed to full and continued cooperation and to provide a report addressing all third-party intermediary transactions as well as the implementation and yearly evaluation of anti-bribery compliance procedures and controls for the duration of the DPA.[30]

It is worth setting out at length the reasons why a DPA was deemed to be in the interests of justice in this instance. Leveson P identified relevant factors as follows:

> the seriousness of the predicate offence or offences; the importance of incentivising the exposure and self-reporting of corporate wrongdoing; the

---

[28] Criminal Law Act 1977, s.1.
[29] Bribery Act 2010, s.7.
[30] *SFO v XYZ Ltd*, Southwark Crown Court, Case No: U20150856, July 8, 2016, para. 14.

history (or otherwise) of similar conduct; the attention paid to corporate compliance prior to, at the time of and subsequent to the offending; the extent to which the entity has changed both in its culture and in relation to relevant personnel; and the impact of prosecution on employees and others innocent of any misconduct.[31]

In relation to seriousness, it was said that 'there is no doubt that XYZ's systematic bribery over a period of eight years was grave'.[32] Of the 74 contracts that were examined as part of this investigation, there was evidence to suggest that 28 of these were procured as a result of the offer or payment of bribes.[33] However, Leveson P then noted that the majority of bribes were instigated by agents who were not under pressure from XYZ. He continued:

> Of particular importance, reflecting a core purpose of the creation of DPAs to incentivise the exposure and self-reporting of corporate wrongdoing, was the promptness of the self-report, the fully disclosed internal investigation and co-operation of XYZ.[34]

Another key consideration was that the corporate had subsequently implemented new training programmes, policies and procedures (and it was this implementation that led to the discovery of the conduct in question). Also, the parent company would not profit from XYZ's criminality; there was nothing to suggest that the parent company should have known about the conduct; and there was no suggestion the XYZ was deliberately operated as a vehicle through which corrupt payments might be made.[35] An important consideration for Leveson P was an economic one:

> prosecution and conviction would lead to significant legal costs and financial penalty at an unfavourable time in the industry, a context where XYZ currently operates on an 'economic knife-edge': XYZ would risk insolvency harming the interests of workers, suppliers, and the wider community.

---

[31] Ibid., para. 15.
[32] Ibid., para. 16.
[33] Ibid., para. 7.
[34] Ibid., para. 16.
[35] Ibid., para. 17.

In any event, it is clear that XYZ in its current form is effectively a different entity from that which committed the offence.[36]

Taking the above into consideration, it was deemed that a DPA was in the interests of justice.

Key Issue in the 'XYZ Ltd' Case

There are a number of issues raised in this case that merit further discussion. First, to what extent should the corporate's ability to pay be taken into consideration?

> At what level of criminality is it necessary simply to allow the SME to become insolvent and to what extent is it appropriate to mitigate the financial penalty, knowing that the SME is only able to make any substantial payment with the support of the substantial company of which the SME is a wholly owned subsidiary? On the one hand, allowing the SME to continue to trade (assuming necessary compliance has been put in place) is in the public interest but, on the other hand, nothing must be done to encourage the pursuit of criminal behaviour through a corporate vehicle which can be abandoned as insolvent if necessary.[37]

It is useful to set out the considerations that influenced the financial terms of the DPA. It was emphasised at the outset that the disgorgement and financial penalty figures 'were determined in a context where XYZ has limited means and ability such that the maximum amount it would be able to provide towards paying any financial obligation imposed without becoming insolvent is estimated to be £352,000'.[38] The total gross profit from the implicated contracts was £6,553,085.[39] As noted above, the total financial orders imposed in this instance was £6,553,085—that is, the equivalent to the gross profit. The total financial orders, then, can be contrasted with those in the Standard Bank DPA, and indeed in subsequent DPAs involving Rolls Royce and Tesco (discussed below).

---

[36] Ibid., para. 18.

[37] *SFO v XYZ Limited, Preliminary DPA Judgment*, Southwark Crown Court, Case No: U20150856, July 8, 2016, para. 3.

[38] *SFO v XYZ Ltd*, Southwark Crown Court, Case No: U20150856, July 8, 2016, para. 20.

[39] Ibid., para. 9.

Looking at the rationale here: while the culpability starting point was high, the parties submitted a (lower than expected) harm multiplier figure of 250%.[40] Applying this figure (i.e. 250% of the gross profit £6,553,085), the starting point for a financial penalty would be almost £16.4 million. In applying a discount for a guilty plea, Leveson P reduced the figure to £8.2 million: it was felt that 'a discount of 50% was appropriate not least to encourage others to conduct themselves as XYZ has when confronting criminality'.[41] This 50% discount is significant: not only is it higher than the 30% discount in the Standard Bank case, it has been welcomed as a necessary approach to incentivise corporates to self-report.[42] While Leveson P's intentions were clear,[43] such a discount feeds concern that corporates receive preferential treatment compared to individual wrongdoers.

Even with the 50% discount, the figure was said to be 'wholly unrealistic' for XYZ; Leveson P then went on to consider 'all the circumstances'[44]—again here the economic considerations weigh heavily in the judgment. The considerations included:

> the conclusion that the interests of justice did not require XYZ to be pursued into insolvency. Thus, XYZ's means and the impact of any financial

---

[40] Even then, it was noted that the multiplier figure 'was always going to be academic given XYZ's means and ability to pay'. Ibid., para. 23.

[41] Ibid.

[42] Lloyd Firth, 'The UK's Second DPA: A Hopeful Judgment', *Economia* (July 25, 2016), available at: http://economia.icaew.com/features/july-2016/the-uks-second-dpa-a-hopeful-judgment (last accessed January 17, 2018). It is also noted that the US DOJ now makes provision for a 50% discount in FCPA enforcement actions: US Department of Justice, 'Memo: The Fraud Section's Foreign Corrupt Practices Act Enforcement Plan and Guidance' (April 5, 2016) section B2 'Credit for Voluntary Self-Disclosure, Full Cooperation, and Timely and Appropriate Remediation in FCPA Matters'.

[43] Referring to CJA 2003, s.144 and the sentencing guidelines, he stated: 'Given the self-report and admission, under the guideline, a full reduction of one third is justified and appropriate. In addition, given that the admissions are far in advance of the first reasonable opportunity having been charged and brought before the court, that discount can be increased as representing additional mitigation. In the circumstances, a discount of 50% could be appropriate not least to encourage others how to conduct themselves when confronting criminality as XYZ has'. *SFO v XYZ Limited, Preliminary DPA Judgment*, Southwark Crown Court, Case No: U20150856, July 8, 2016, para. 57.

[44] *SFO v XYZ Ltd*, Southwark Crown Court, Case No: U20150856, July 8, 2016, para. 24.

penalty on XYZ's staff, service users, customers and the local economy are all significant factors. SFO accountants accept that £352,000 is a reasonable estimate of the sum that will be available to XYZ to provide towards any financial obligations and that the balance would have to be provided through support from ABC. As a result, taking into account the sum to be disgorged of £6,201,085, a financial penalty of £352,000 leads to a total which equates to the gross profit on the implicated contracts.[45]

It was noted that the amounts of the disgorgement order and the financial penalty could have been increased/reduced in equal measure, with the overall amount remaining the same. Ultimately, Leveson P stated: 'The pragmatic answer is that, in these circumstances, the overall sum payable (whether called disgorgement or financial penalty) sufficiently marks the offending and is itself fair, reasonable and proportionate'.[46] According to the SFO Director, David Green, '[t]he decision as to whether to force a company into insolvency must be balanced with the level and nature of co-operation and this case provides a clear example to corporates'.[47] A clear message has been communicated to corporates here that if they can demonstrate a risk of insolvency alongside full cooperation in the investigation then this will in turn represent a mitigating factor even in those cases where the criminality is systematic, extensive and repetitive. It is difficult to imagine a scenario where full, exemplary cooperation would not be offered following a self-report (as happened here).

As an aside, it is worth noting that the SFO agreed not to seek costs in light of XYZ's means and ability to pay.[48] Moreover, a compensation order 'was not appropriate as it was not possible to positively identify any victims as entities who may be compensated'.[49]

A second, and related, issue is the role of the parent company in the DPA process. In this instance, ABC had offered to provide necessary financial support in the event that a DPA was to be agreed, even though 'there was neither contractual nor legal obligation on ABC, as an innocent parent company, to contribute towards a financial penalty imposed

---

[45] Ibid.
[46] Ibid.
[47] SFO, 'Press Release—SFO Secures Second DPA' (July 8, 2016).
[48] *SFO v XYZ Ltd*, Southwark Crown Court, Case No: U20150856, July 8, 2016, para. 25.
[49] Ibid., para. 20.

upon one of its subsidiaries for criminal conduct by that subsidiary'.[50] If a subsidiary is prosecuted and unable to pay the penalty imposed, then it can be wound up. But, as counsel for XYZ accepted, 'a parent company receiving financial benefits arising from the unlawful conduct of a subsidiary (albeit unknown) must understand how this will be perceived'.[51] ABC had in fact received £6 million in dividends from XYZ since acquiring it in 2000. It was agreed between XYZ and ABC that, as well as providing financial support to meet the terms of the DPA, ABC would also return £1,953,085 of these dividends to XYZ.[52] In concluding, Leveson P stated:

> Before parting from this case, I must underline one further point. ABC was entirely ignorant of what had been happening at XYZ and its conduct when it had intimation of the facts has been beyond reproach. Its behaviour and its support for XYZ have been important features in allowing the case to be resolved in the way in which it has.[53]

He re-iterated:

> ... it is important to send a clear message, reflecting a policy choice in bringing DPAs into the law of England and Wales, that a company's shareholders, customers and employees (as well as all those with whom it deals) are far better served by self-reporting and putting in place effective compliance structures. When it does so, that openness must be rewarded and be seen to be worthwhile.[54]

Where, however, there is evidence that a subsidiary is established as a vehicle through which corrupt payments may be made (and can be abandoned in the event of prosecution), then a parent company itself will likely face prosecution under section 7 of the Bribery Act. It was emphasised that 'A preexisting plan to behave corruptly through the subsidiary would obviously be treated as a seriously aggravating feature'.[55]

---

[50] Ibid., para. 21.
[51] Ibid.
[52] Ibid., para. 22.
[53] Ibid., para. 28.
[54] Ibid., referring to the preliminary DPA judgment at para. 45.
[55] Ibid., para. 28.

A third issue to consider is that, alongside the DPA, there would be prosecution of individuals (which is why the DPA judgment remains redacted). From the perspective of the corporate, such a proposition might be attractive in that it avoids drawn-out negative publicity:

> This has allowed XYZ a temporary anonymity which, if it were to become the norm for DPA proceedings, would certainly be attractive to companies wanting to avoid a drawn out process in the public eye, in favour of one short burst of negative publicity when the prosecution of the individuals is complete.[56]

While XYZ has not attracted the same level of attention as other DPAs—the Rolls Royce one in particular—it is clear that there are significant issues to be taken from the approach adopted here. Indeed, it further supports the idea that the SFO is receptive to negotiated non-contention[57]—'XYZ does suggest that the SFO is willing to take a more commercial approach than the "prosecutor first and foremost" rhetoric would tend to suggest'.[58] Moreover, it confirms that DPAs are not confined to larger corporates (where criminal prosecution is difficult); XYZ is an SME.

Case 3—Rolls Royce

Of the DPAs concluded to date, the one with Rolls Royce has been the most notable, not least in terms of the size and significance of the company, but also in terms of the issues that have been raised. In January

---

[56] Thomas Webb, 'The Serious Fraud Office Has Its Second Deferred Prosecution Agreement Approved', Burges Salmon News and Insight (August 25, 2016), available at: https://www.burges-salmon.com/news-and-insight/legal-updates/the-serious-fraud-office-has-its-second-deferred-prosecution-agreement-approved/ (last accessed January 17, 2017).

[57] Nicholas Lord and Colin King, 'Negotiating Non-contention: Civil Recovery and Deferred Prosecution in Response to Transnational Corporate Bribery', in Liz Campbell and Nicholas Lord (eds), *Corruption in Commercial Enterprise: Law, Theory and Practice* (Routledge, 2018).

[58] Quinton Newcomb, 'Second UK DPA Betrays a Commercial Approach by the SFO Despite the Tough "Prosecute First" Rhetoric', Fulcrum Chambers—General News (July 13, 2016), available at: http://www.fulcrumchambers.com/deferred-prosecution-agreements/ (last accessed January 17, 2018).

2017, the SFO secured approval from Lord Justice Leveson for its third DPA, with Rolls Royce PLC, involving 12 counts of conspiracy to corrupt, false accounting and failure to prevent bribery. The company, specifically its Civil Aerospace and Defence Aerospace businesses and its former Energy business, used a network of agents to bribe officials in at least seven different countries[59] to win lucrative contracts over a period spanning three decades—the profit gained was evaluated to be £258,170,000.[60] Consequently, the company agreed a financial settlement of £497.25 million (comprising of a disgorgement of the profit gained plus a financial penalty of £239,082,645 in addition to £12,960,754 prosecution costs)[61] with the SFO.[62] As with the earlier DPAs, it was also explicitly made clear that no tax reduction would be sought in relation to these payments. The DPA spans a 5-year term and also involves an agreement to cooperate with and assist the SFO with the prosecution of individual company actors as well as the implementation of a compliance programme that is to be supervised by Lord Gold.

In approving the DPA, Leveson P stated:

> it can properly be described as devastating and of the very greatest gravity that the conduct of this institution should fall to be examined within the context of a criminal investigation and that the investigation … should reveal the most serious breaches of the criminal law in the areas of bribery and corruption (some of which implicated senior management and, on the face of it, controlling minds of the company).[63]

At the outset, then, it is important to consider the reasons why a DPA was deemed to be in the interests of justice. It is axiomatic that the conduct in question was of a serious nature. Moreover, there were aggravating factors including (1) The offences related to bribery of foreign public

---

[59] Indonesia, Thailand, India, Russia, Nigeria, China and Malaysia.

[60] SFO Press Release, SFO completes £497.25 million Deferred Prosecution Agreement with Rolls-Royce plc (January 17, 2017).

[61] *SFO v Rolls Royce PLC; Rolls Royce Energy Systems Inc*, Southwark Crown Court, Case No: U20170036, January 17, 2017, para. 67.

[62] Rolls-Royce also reached agreements with the US Department of Justice and Brazil's Ministério Público Federal. These agreements result in the payment of US$169,917,710 and $25,579,645, respectively, to the US and Brazilian authorities. Ibid., para. 69.

[63] *SFO v Rolls Royce PLC; Rolls Royce Energy Systems Inc*, Southwark Crown Court, Case No: U20170036, January 17, 2017, para. 4.

officials, commercial bribery and false accounting of payments to intermediaries; (2) The offences were multi-jurisdictional and spread across different Rolls Royce businesses; (3) The offences have caused (and/or will cause) harm to the integrity and confidence of markets; (4) The offending was persistent (spanning 1989–2013); (5) Substantial funds were used to fund bribery; (6) The conduct displayed elements of careful planning; (7) The conduct related to the award of large value contracts; and (8) The conduct involved senior Rolls Royce employees.[64] What, then, were the 'strong countervailing considerations'[65] justifying a DPA in this case?

First, notwithstanding the lack of a self-report, Rolls Royce was said to have been extremely co-operative in the investigation. Indeed, from the moment that concerns were raised, Leveson P noted, 'the company could not have done more to expose its own misconduct'.[66] He continued: 'incentivising self-reporting is a core purpose of DPAs and the weight it attracts depends on the totality of the information provided. In one sense, the more egregious the conduct, the greater significance of wholesale self-reporting and admission: the question is to identify the tipping point'.[67] Leveson P also acknowledged the costs of the work undertaken by Rolls Royce (in cooperating with investigators as well as paying for professional financial advice), which amounted to £123,115,643 as of December 2016.[68]

Second, in relation to prior conduct, the judge did refer to previous instances of wrongdoing, but opined that they were not relevant to the present case. More relevant, it was said, were the US DPA with the DOJ and the leniency agreement with the Brazilian Ministério Público Federal, which concerned similar conduct to that at issue in the UK DPA application. Leveson P then stated:

> A DPA should not become wrong simply because different prosecutors have been involved in investigations in different countries although it is right to observe that the extension of the criminality to these countries is relevant to the balancing exercise.[69]

---

[64] Ibid., para. 35.
[65] Ibid.
[66] Ibid., para. 38.
[67] Ibid.
[68] Ibid., para. 39.
[69] Ibid., para. 42.

Third, Leveson P acknowledged the corporate compliance steps taken by Rolls Royce after the offending, which cost £15,175,331.46 as of December 2016.[70] While he did 'entirely accept that Rolls-Royce could not have done more to address the issues that have now been exposed', he then emphasised: 'it is a real tragedy that it did not do so following the well-known observations of Kofi Annan, in the foreword to the 2004 UN Convention against Corruption which spoke about it as "an insidious plague"'.[71]

Fourth, the change of culture and personnel was emphasised:

> Had any member of the today's senior management who was implicated or been in a position where they should have been aware of the culture and practices which I have described and were clearly endemic at Rolls-Royce remained in his or her position, this, itself, would have been of real significance and could have affected my approach.[72]

Leveson P concluded: 'I am satisfied that both the senior management and those responsible for the strategic direction of Rolls-Royce are different to those responsible for the running of the company (and its culture) during the period when the events which I have described occurred'.[73]

Fifth, the consequences of a criminal conviction were considered, including the ability of Rolls Royce to trade globally (e.g. due to debarment rules), loss of revenue, loss of contracts, reduced research and development, impact on the financial position of Rolls Royce, and repercussions for third parties.[74] Leveson P stated: 'a criminal conviction against Rolls-Royce would have a very substantial impact on the company, which, in turn, would have wider effects for the UK defence industry and persons who were not connected to the criminal conduct, including Rolls-Royce employees, and pensioners, and those in its supply chain'.[75] He then continued:

---

[70] Ibid., para. 47.
[71] Ibid.
[72] Ibid., para. 48.
[73] Ibid., para. 51.
[74] See ibid., paras. 52–56.
[75] Ibid., para. 57.

None of these factors is determinative of my decision in relation to this DPA; indeed, the national economic interest is irrelevant. Neither is my decision founded on the proposition that a company in the position of Rolls-Royce is immune from prosecution: it is not. It is not because of who or what Rolls-Royce is that is relevant but, rather, the countervailing factors that I have to weigh in the balance when considering the public interest and the interests of justice. As I have made clear before, and repeat, a company that commits serious crimes must expect to be prosecuted and if convicted dealt with severely and, absent sufficient countervailing factors, cannot expect to have an application for approval of a DPA accepted.[76]

A sixth consideration, which was raised by the SFO, was that 'the proposed DPA would avoid the significant expenditure of time and money which would be inherent in any prosecution of Rolls-Royce'.[77] It was emphasised that this investigation was the largest ever undertaken by the SFO.

Although the SFO is ready and able to prosecute large corporates like Rolls-Royce, where necessary, its resources (both financial and in terms of manpower) are not unlimited so that when an agreement such as this can be negotiated, the public interest requires consideration to be given to the cases that will not be investigated if very substantial resources (sufficient to prepare the case for a hearing) are diverted to it.[78]

The seventh, and final, consideration—also raised by the SFO, and one that relates to dicta of Leveson P in the earlier DPAs—relates to incentivising corporates to self-report. Leveson P stated: 'This is of vital importance in the context of the investigation and prosecution of complex corruption cases in bringing more information to the attention of law enforcement agencies so that crimes can be properly investigated, and prosecuted effectively'.[79] Moreover, it was said that 'the effect of the DPA is to require the company concerned to become a flagship of good practice and an example to others demonstrating what can be done to ensure ethical good practice in the business world'.[80]

[76] Ibid.
[77] Ibid., para. 58.
[78] Ibid.
[79] Ibid., para. 60.
[80] Ibid., para. 60.

In considering the interests of justice, and after detailing the above considerations, Leveson P stated:

> My reaction when first considering these papers was that *if Rolls-Royce were not to be prosecuted in the context of such egregious criminality over decades*, involving countries around the world, making truly vast corrupt payments and, consequentially, even greater profits, *then it was difficult to see when any company would be prosecuted.* (emphasis added)[81]

That notwithstanding,

> I accept that Rolls-Royce is no longer the company that once it was; its new Board and executive team has embraced the need to make essential change and has deliberately sought to clear out all the disreputable practices that have gone before, creating new policies, practices and cultures. Its full co-operation and willingness to expose every potential criminal act that it uncovers and the work being done on compliance and creating that culture goes a long way to address the obvious concerns as to the past.[82]

Ultimately, for Leveson P, 'the question becomes whether it is necessary to inflict the undeniably adverse consequences on Rolls-Royce that would flow from prosecution because of the gravity of its offending even though it may now be considered a dramatically changed organisation'.[83] Leveson P concluded that a DPA would, in the circumstances, be appropriate.

Key Issues in the Rolls Royce Case

While welcomed by some,[84] the Rolls Royce DPA has been criticised by others, including the NGO Corruption Watch who labelled it

---

[81] Ibid., para. 61.
[82] Ibid., para. 62.
[83] Ibid., para. 63.

[84] For example, it has been said that: 'This is a sensible and expedient decision, where the court weighed up complex and conflicting factors to arrive at a conclusion that, on balance, was in the public interest'. Osborne Clarke, 'The Rolls-Royce DPA: What Is the Message for Other Businesses?', available at: http://www.osborneclarke.com/insights/the-rolls-royce-dpa-what-is-the-message-for-other-businesses/ (last accessed January 30, 2018).

'a failure of nerve'.[85] We now turn to consider some of the key issues arising from this DPA.

First, the seriousness of the conduct at issue—which was said to include 'the most serious breaches of the criminal law in the areas of bribery and corruption'[86]—is arguably a matter that should be dealt with by criminal prosecution, rather than a negotiated settlement. Indeed, as Leveson P explicitly recognised, if Rolls Royce was not prosecuted in this instance, then it is difficult to see when a corporate would be prosecuted.[87] The DPA Code of Practice states:

> The more serious the offence, the more likely it is that prosecution will be required in the public interest. Indicators of seriousness include not just the value of any gain or loss, but also the risk of harm to the public, to unidentified victims, shareholders, employees and creditors and to the stability and integrity of financial markets and international trade. The impact of the offending in other countries, and not just the consequences in the UK, should be taken into account.[88]

The factors that were said to justify a DPA resolution in this instance are debateable: cooperation by the corporate is a factor that ought to be recognised at the sentencing stage, rather than enabling the corporate to avoid prosecution. Giving the corporate credit for improving compliance fails to recognise that the corporate should already have had in place adequate procedures, particularly in relation to those offences taking place *after* the introduction of the Bribery Act 2010 and the explicit focus on 'failure to prevent'. Similarly with the change in culture and personnel, that is something that ought to be expected in the wake of such egregious wrongdoing, not something that should be a factor against prosecution. Again here,

---

[85] Corruption Watch, 'A Failure of Nerve: The SFO's Settlement with Rolls Royce' (January 19, 2017), available at: http://www.cw-uk.org/2017/01/19/a-failure-of-nerve-the-sfos-settlement-with-rolls-royce/ (last accessed January 28, 2018).

[86] *SFO v Rolls Royce PLC; Rolls Royce Energy Systems Inc*, Southwark Crown Court, Case No: U20170036, January 17, 2017, para. 4.

[87] *SFO v Rolls Royce PLC; Rolls Royce Energy Systems Inc*, Southwark Crown Court, Case No: U20170036, January 17, 2017, para. 61.

[88] SFO/CPS, *Deferred Prosecution Agreements Code of Practice* (2013), para. 2.4.

5 DEFERRED PROSECUTION AGREEMENTS: IN PRACTICE   103

both of these changes might be reflected at sentencing stage following conviction, as opposed to avoiding prosecution. Furthermore, Leveson P was influenced by the consequences of a criminal conviction. Yet, he later stated that 'As for the non-penal consequences of conviction, the purpose of the procurement rules is specifically to discourage corruption and they should not be circumvented'.[89] In addition, this reinforces concern that there is one rule for corporates and another for individual wrongdoers—where the consequences of conviction tend to be reserved for the sentencing stage (this issue is discussed further in Chapter 6). Indeed, while Leveson P noted that a corporate such as Rolls Royce is not immune from prosecution, and that 'a company that commits serious crimes must expect to be prosecuted and if convicted dealt with severely',[90] such sentiments ring rather hollow given how Rolls Royce did in fact avoid prosecution (notwithstanding the financial penalties, discussed below).[91] Moreover, while consideration was given to the impact on Rolls Royce, its employees and shareholders who would be affected in the event of criminal prosecution,

> no reference was made to the victims of the corruption that Rolls Royce committed. None of the prosecuting authorities from the countries where bribes were paid appear to have been given a right to make representations to the court. And no real assessment of the potential harm caused by Rolls Royce's corruption appears to have been made by the SFO. Such corruption undermines democracy, the rule of law and socio-economic development, disadvantaging citizens in victim countries.[92]

---

[89] *SFO v Rolls Royce PLC; Rolls Royce Energy Systems Inc*, Southwark Crown Court, Case No: U20170036, January 17, 2017, para. 61. It has also been suggested that the adverse consequences of conviction were 'vastly overplayed and their consideration as a public interest factor against prosecution undermines government commitments to ensure corrupt bidders are excluded from public contracts'. Corruption Watch, 'A Failure of Nerve: The SFO's Settlement with Rolls Royce' (January 19, 2017), available at: http://www.cw-uk.org/2017/01/19/a-failure-of-nerve-the-sfos-settlement-with-rolls-royce/ (last accessed January 28, 2018).

[90] *SFO v Rolls Royce PLC; Rolls Royce Energy Systems Inc*, Southwark Crown Court, Case No: U20170036, January 17, 2017, para. 57.

[91] This assumes, of course, that the corporate will satisfy all the terms of the DPA during the period that the prosecution is deferred.

[92] Corruption Watch, 'A Failure of Nerve: The SFO's Settlement with Rolls Royce' (January 19, 2017), available at: http://www.cw-uk.org/2017/01/19/a-failure-of-nerve-the-sfos-settlement-with-rolls-royce/ (last accessed January 28, 2018).

Furthermore, the consideration that entering into a DPA with Rolls Royce would be beneficial from the SFO's perspective, as well as in the public interest—on the basis that it 'would avoid the significant expenditure of time and money which would be inherent in any prosecution of Rolls-Royce'[93]—is concerning. Surely the SFO did not mean to imply that the bigger the corporate under investigation, and the more complex the case, the more they would be open to settlement. If decisions to prosecute are influenced by what the authorities can afford, this raises concerns over the message being communicated to the business community. (Unless cost to the taxpayer is a valid reason for prosecution not being in the public interest.)[94] Finally, the emphasis on incentivising corporates to self-report by entering into this DPA reinforces concern that corporates are being differentially treated. As noted in Chapter 2, an individual who cooperates with an investigation is likely to receive a discount at sentencing stage (i.e. she will still be convicted), whereas the corporate criminal will avoid conviction as a result of cooperation.

Second, the size of the financial penalty must be emphasised. The initial penalty—prior to any discount—was £478,165,290.[95] After a discount (of 50%, discussed below) was applied for Rolls Royce's cooperation, the total penalty figure was £239,082,645. Added to this was the disgorgement of profit of £258,170,000. As Leveson P emphasised, 'Public policy favours the removal of any benefit from crime and Rolls-Royce and RRESI have the means and ability to pay'.[96] Thus, the total amount payable was £497,252,645, plus SFO costs of £12,960,754.[97]

---

[93] *SFO v Rolls Royce PLC; Rolls Royce Energy Systems Inc*, Southwark Crown Court, Case No: U20170036, January 17, 2017, para. 58

[94] It is noticeable that the SFO impressed upon the court that resourcing consideration, particularly in relation to investigations/prosecutions of large corporates, do influence its decisions whether to proceed with a case, and that in such situations it is open to negotiation. Ibid., para. 58.

[95] Ibid., para. 118.

[96] Ibid., para. 75. It was stressed, though, that 'care must be used in relation to this term [i.e. gross profit] which is based on calculations reached by accountants instructed by the SFO and Rolls-Royce and agreed by the parties and does not necessarily reflect the way in which the accounting profession would approach gross profit for reporting standards'. Ibid., para. 35. For consideration of how disgorgement was calculated for the different counts, see para. 74 *et seq.*

[97] Ibid., paras. 123–125.

Table 5.1 Overall calculation (Rolls Royce DPA)[a]

Count[b]	Gross profit for disgorgement (£)	Gross profit as basis of fine (£)	Multiplier	Harm penalty (£)	Equivalent guilty plea discount (%)	Effect of discount (£)	Additional extraordinary cooperation discount (%)	Effect of additional discount (£)	Total payment (£)
1	30,330,000.00	30,330,000.00	3.25	98,572,500.00	33.3	65,747,857.50	16.7	49,286,250.00	79,616,250.00
2, 3, 4	118,150,000.00	39,500,000.00	4	158,000,000.00	33.3	105,386,000.00	16.7	79,000,000.00	197,150,000.00
5	7,890,000.00	7,890,000.00	2.5	19,725,000.00	33.3	13,156,575.00	16.7	9,862,500.00	17,752,500.00
6	–	1,850,000.00	3.25	6,012,500.00	33.3	4,010,337.50	16.7	3,006,250.00	3,006,250.00
7	36,800,000.00	36,800,000.00	3.25	119,600,000.00	33.3	79,773,200.00	16.7	59,800,000.00	96,600,000.00
8	2,860,000.00	–	–	–	–	–	16.7	–	2,860,000.00
9	–	7,055,000.00	2.5	17,637,500.00	33.3	11,764,212.50	16.7	8,818,750.00	8,818,750.00
10	13,960,000.00	–	–	–	33.3	–	16.7	–	13,960,000.00
11	31,100,000.00	20,713,000.00	2.83	58,617,790.00	33.3	39,098,065.93	16.7	29,308,895.00	60,408,895.00
12	17,080,000.00	–	–	–	33.3	–	16.7	–	17,080,000.00
Total financial sanction[c]	258,170,000.00	144,138,000.00		478,165,290.00	33.3	318,936,248.43	16.7	239,082,645.00	497,252,645.00

[a]Adapted from *SFO v Rolls Royce PLC; Rolls Royce Energy Systems Inc*, Southwark Crown Court, Case No: U20170036, January 17, 2017, Appendix B. Added to the monetary sanctions specified here were costs of £12,960,754.00

[b]A summary of facts and of each count is contained in Appendix A of the DPA judgment

[c]For a monetary breakdown of each count, see *SFO v Rolls Royce PLC; Rolls Royce Energy Systems Inc*, Southwark Crown Court, Case No: U20170036, January 17, 2017, para. 85 *et seq*

Table 5.1 details the breakdown across the different counts faced by Rolls Royce.

Even putting aside any reputational damage, it was said that 'the total financial impact ... achieves the objectives of punishment and deterrence'.[98] While the size of the financial penalties is substantial, compared to other fines levied in the UK (but not the US), we must question further whether the objectives of punishment and deterrence have indeed been achieved. Empirical research on deterrence indicates that it is the certainty of punishment, not the severity of punishment, that is the core factor in effective deterrence.[99] In other words, it is the 'apprehension probability' that affects levels of deterrence.[100] Where detection for serious corporate financial crimes is largely reliant on self-reports as we see with foreign bribery, this implies that the likelihood of apprehension remains low. The SFO is seeking to be more proactive in detection through 'massive' expansion of its intelligence capabilities (e.g. information from insiders, competitors or disgruntled spouses).[101] However, such intelligence gathering must receive adequate resourcing.[102] By increasing the likelihood of detection in this way, corporates can be incentivised to self-report—if they fail to notify the SFO of potential bribery when they come across it, they run the risk of the SFO identifying it first and this, according to the DPA policy, can reduce the likelihood of being invited for DPA negotiations. The low likelihood of detection is further reinforced given that financial penalties for bribery—in those cases that are detected—can be straightforwardly subsumed by the corporate as a cost of business, though attempts at proportionality are clear as profits gained are disgorged. That said, it could be argued that in the absence of credible incapacitation mechanisms, the enforced regime change as part of DPA terms may be rehabilitative and therefore crime reductive. However, questions remain over the retributive dimension to such penalties—did Rolls Royce receive 'just deserts'?

---

[98] Ibid., para. 127.

[99] Daniel S. Nagin, 'Deterrence in the Twenty-First Century', *Crime and Justice* (2013), 42(1): 199.

[100] Ibid., p. 202.

[101] Christopher Williams, 'Britain's Anti-fraud Chief David Green Battles the Critics and City Wrongdoing', *The Telegraph* (April 9, 2016).

[102] OECD, *Implementing the OECD Anti-bribery Convention. Phase 4 Report: United Kingdom* (OECD, 2017), p. 17.

Furthermore, this case, as with others, lacks credible restoration as victims remain unidentified.

Third, this case represents 'an interesting exception to the rule that a self-report is a precondition for a DPA'[103] In both the previous two DPAs (Standard Bank and XYZ Ltd, discussed above) 'the DPA followed what was a self-report at a time that the SFO neither had knowledge of, nor known means of likelihood of learning about, the conduct which led to the DPA'.[104] In this instance, the SFO investigation was triggered by a whistleblower, rather than by a self-report.[105] Notwithstanding, once concerns were raised Rolls Royce was said to have been extremely cooperative in the investigation.[106] Leveson P noted that the absence of a self-report

> would usually be highly relevant in the balance [i.e. between prosecution and DPA] but the nature and extent of the co-operation provided by Rolls-Royce in this case has persuaded the SFO not only to use the word "extraordinary" to describe it but also to advance the argument that, in the particular circumstances of this case, I should not distinguish between its assistance and that of those who have self-reported from the outset. Given that what has been reported has clearly been far more extensive (and of a different order) than is may have been exposed without the co-operation provided, I am prepared to accede to that submission.[107]

Indeed, Leveson P concluded that—given the extent of cooperation—a reduction of 50% would be appropriate in the circumstances, which is discussed next. The conclusion that a corporate can be offered a DPA notwithstanding the absence of a self-report has, however, been criticised. In a scathing commentary on this agreement, Corruption Watch stated:

---

[103] Ibid., p. 16.

[104] *SFO v Rolls Royce PLC; Rolls Royce Energy Systems Inc*, Southwark Crown Court, Case No: U20170036, January 17, 2017, para. 21.

[105] See ibid, para. 16, where it is noted that concerns were first raised in internet postings.

[106] See ibid, paras. 17–20. Indeed, counsel for the SFO recognised 'the extraordinary cooperation of Rolls-Royce' (para. 19).

[107] Ibid., para. 22.

The Rolls Royce DPA, therefore, sets a precedent that a company can fail to disclose – in fact deliberately decide not to disclose information about wrongdoing …, but if it then cooperates with the SFO it will still be eligible for a DPA. Companies will heave a sigh of relief that they can now safely take the risk of not disclosing wrongdoing to the SFO, but still receive all the advantages of a DPA if they do get caught as long as they then play ball. This DPA therefore potentially undermines incentives for companies to self-report – a key plank of why DPAs were introduced.[108]

Following Rolls Royce, it is not clear where Leveson P's 'tipping point'[109] is, in relation to when a DPA is possible absent a self-report. This also raises the concern that rational, amoral corporates would choose not to self-report if full cooperation once detected is sufficient to enter into negotiations for a DPA.

Fourth, the 'generous reduction in sentence granted by the Court raises a question about incentives for self-reporting'.[110] Rolls Royce received a discount of 50% (following the approach in XYZ Ltd), notwithstanding that there was no self-report in this instance. Indeed, in the US—where a separate DPA was agreed with Rolls Royce—the discount was 25%.[111] Moreover, in XYZ Ltd, it had been said 'given that the admissions are far in advance of the first reasonable opportunity having been charged and brought before the court, that discount can be increased as representing additional mitigation'.[112] It was noted that the discount of 50% was appropriate 'not least to encourage others how to conduct themselves when confronting criminality as XYZ has'.[113]

---

[108] Corruption Watch, 'A Failure of Nerve: The SFO's Settlement with Rolls Royce' (January 19, 2017), available at: http://www.cw-uk.org/2017/01/19/a-failure-of-nerve-the-sfos-settlement-with-rolls-royce/ (last accessed January 28, 2018).

[109] *SFO v Rolls Royce PLC; Rolls Royce Energy Systems Inc*, Southwark Crown Court, Case No: U20170036, January 17, 2017, para. 38.

[110] OECD, *Implementing the OECD Anti-Bribery Convention. Phase 4 Report: United Kingdom* (OECD, 2017), p. 16.

[111] OECD, *Implementing the OECD Anti-Bribery Convention. Phase 4 Report: United Kingdom* (OECD, 2017), p. 17. For details of the US DPA, see Department of Justice, Press Release—Rolls Royce plc Agrees to Pay $170 Million Criminal Penalty to Resolve Foreign Corrupt Practices Act Case (January 17, 2017).

[112] *SFO v XYZ Limited, Preliminary DPA Judgment*, Southwark Crown Court, Case No: U20150856, July 8, 2016, para. 57.

[113] Ibid.

In the Rolls Royce case there was no self-report, but the additional discount was applied on the basis of the 'extraordinary cooperation' demonstrated by Rolls Royce.[114] Not only does this discount have the potential to undermine incentives for corporates to self-report in the future,[115] it also 'raised questions about who Leveson is accountable to when changing DPA policy on such a fundamental basis'.[116] Moreover, the discount of 50% is actually higher than the corporate would likely have received if it had been criminally prosecuted and pleaded guilty at an early stage.

Fifth, the SFO provided assurances to Rolls Royce that 'on approval of the DPA, it would not consider it to be in the interests of justice to investigate or prosecute it for additional conduct pre-dating the DPA and arising from the currently opened investigations into Airbus and Unaoil (which, in any event, is covered by the deferred prosecution agreement reached by Rolls-Royce in the United States)'.[117] This is a problematic scenario as the integrity, and legitimacy, of the DPA is brought into question given the essential immunity it offers for other analogous bribery associated with Rolls Royce. Given the extensive and full cooperation by Rolls Royce, it might be expected that their internal investigations, if carried out diligently, would have determined

---

[114] *SFO v Rolls Royce PLC; Rolls Royce Energy Systems Inc*, Southwark Crown Court, Case No: U20170036, January 17, 2017, para. 121.

[115] OECD, *Implementing the OECD Anti-Bribery Convention. Phase 4 Report: United Kingdom* (OECD, 2017), p. 17.

[116] Corruption Watch, 'A Failure of Nerve: The SFO's Settlement with Rolls Royce' (January 19, 2017), available at: http://www.cw-uk.org/2017/01/19/a-failure-of-nerve-the-sfos-settlement-with-rolls-royce/ (last accessed January 28, 2018).

[117] *SFO v Rolls Royce PLC; Rolls Royce Energy Systems Inc*, Southwark Crown Court, Case No: U20170036, January 17, 2017, para. 134. 'The reason for this conclusion is that the conduct resolved by the DPA spans eight jurisdictions, three of Rolls-Royce's business divisions and over 20 years of conduct. The geographic, commercial and chronological scope together with the quantum of proposed financial terms is such that the matters which are the subject of the DPA are sufficiently extensive to satisfy the public interest. The investigations into Unaoil and Airbus are insufficiently advanced so as to provide evidence that could yet be included in a DPA or prosecuted and substantial further investigation would be required before such an eventuality if it were reached at all. Even if it did it is unlikely that the inclusion of additional matters would materially contribute to any change to the proposed terms'. Ibid., para. 135.

the extent of criminality with regards other known allegations, and the SFO to be notified of this. If the self-investigation did not unearth evidence of further bribery, but it later comes to light that they are implicated, then this in itself may be an indicator of inadequate internal procedures. In this case, it would imply poor performance in how enforcement power is exercised by the SFO if they were not able to prosecute. This further reinforces the differential treatment afforded to large corporates.

Sixth, there is provision for the financial orders to be paid in instalments. Rolls Royce requested time for payment, and the SFO accepted that point.[118] However, there has been criticism that the repayment term is 'overly generous', raises doubt as to the deterrent value of DPAs, and could result in DPA financial penalties being regarded as 'a potential cost of doing business'.[119] Notwithstanding, it is not uncommon with respect to 'ordinary crime' for offenders to agree affordable repayment programmes. In fact, this is a sound approach where the offender, whether an individual or business, is under financial pressure. However, Rolls Royce is one of the most profitable corporates in the UK so permitting the company to integrate the financial penalties over time in this way seems unnecessary.

Seventh, the role of the judiciary merits mention. Leveson P stressed that 'there is no question of the parties having reached a private compromise without appropriate independent judicial consideration of the public interest: furthermore, publication of the relevant material now serves to permit public scrutiny of the circumstances and the agreement'.[120] However, the current DPA procedure—whereby all applications to date have been heard by the same judge—has been criticised. Moreover,

---

[118] *SFO v Rolls Royce PLC; Rolls Royce Energy Systems Inc*, Southwark Crown Court, Case No: U20170036, January 17, 2017, para. 128.

[119] Corruption Watch, 'A Failure of Nerve: The SFO's Settlement with Rolls Royce' (January 19, 2017), available at: http://www.cw-uk.org/2017/01/19/a-failure-of-nerve-the-sfos-settlement-with-rolls-royce/ (last accessed January 28, 2018).

[120] *SFO v Rolls Royce PLC; Rolls Royce Energy Systems Inc*, Southwark Crown Court, Case No: U20170036, January 17, 2017, para. 139.

[t]here is no route for third parties to make representations to the court who might have evidence or reasons for questioning why a DPA might not be in the public interest. Sir Brian [Leveson] therefore only ever hears arguments from two parties, the SFO and the company, who are in agreement about the DPA being a good thing.[121]

This is an important point as these interactions take place outside of public oversight and are underpinned by a mutual desire for a non-contentious outcome to the case.

Eight, Leveson P stressed how this case might be instructive to other corporates who have previously engaged in misconduct. He noted that such corporates now have a choice open to them: a responsible company (the term is that used by Leveson P) will engage openly with the SFO.[122] In contrast:

> A cynic (or irresponsible company) might look at the costs which Rolls-Royce have incurred in their own investigation and wonder whether it be more sensible to keep quiet and hope that its conduct does not fall under the eye of the authorities. Quite apart from the total failure to acknowledge the difference between right and wrong, that is to fail to understand that such an approach carries with it cataclysmic risks. Whatever the costs Rolls-Royce have incurred, they are modest compared to the cost of seeking to brazen out an investigation which commences; absent self-disclosure and full co-operation, prosecution would require the attention of the company to be entirely focused on litigation at the expense of whatever business it is trying to conduct and conviction would almost inevitably spell a far greater disaster than has befallen Rolls-Royce.[123]

Although the rhetoric of cataclysm is powerful, as discussed in Chapters 1 and 6, history indicates that corporate prosecutions are very rare. Given the approach adopted in this instance—whereby a 50% discount was given notwithstanding the lack of a self-report—the likelihood is that rational, amoral corporates will choose not to self-report, if they can still avail of a DPA and the full discount through full cooperation *if* they are detected.

---

[121] Corruption Watch, 'A Failure of Nerve: The SFO's Settlement with Rolls Royce' (January 19, 2017), available at: http://www.cw-uk.org/2017/01/19/a-failure-of-nerve-the-sfos-settlement-with-rolls-royce/ (last accessed January 28, 2018).

[122] *SFO v Rolls Royce PLC; Rolls Royce Energy Systems Inc*, Southwark Crown Court, Case No: U20170036, January 17, 2017, para. 142.

[123] Ibid., para. 143.

Case 4—Tesco Stores Ltd

In the case of Tesco Stores Ltd, a wholly owned subsidiary of Tesco Plc, the criminal behaviour did not relate to bribery, but to accounting fraud, or what Tesco more esoterically referred to as 'historic accounting practices' in its press release.[124] The case first came to light in October 2014 when Tesco revealed it had overstated its profits by over £326 million between February and September 2014 in relation to how the company booked payments from its suppliers.[125] These 'accounting irregularities' were discovered 22 days after Dave Lewis took over as the CEO.[126] The SFO opened a criminal investigation into the alleged fraud in October 2014 and in April 2017 confirmed that a DPA had been negotiated with Tesco and again approved by Lord Justice Leveson. In its press release on the DPA, the SFO stated:

> This DPA only relates to the potential criminal liability of Tesco Stores Limited and does not address whether liability of any sort attaches to Tesco Plc or any current or former employee or agent of Tesco Plc or Tesco Stores Ltd.[127]

The ambiguity of this statement reflects the reporting restrictions put in place in order to avoid prejudicing other on-going and related prosecutions against three individuals—Carl Rogberg (Finance Director), Christopher Bush (Managing Director of Tesco's UK operations) and John Scouler (Food Commercial Director). The three are charged with false accounting[128] and fraud by abuse of position,[129] in relation to falsely inflating the grocer's profits in 2014. The trial of these individuals

---

[124] Tesco Plc, 'Press Release—Deferred Prosecution Agreement in Relation to Historic Accounting Practices' (March 28, 2017).

[125] Graham Ruddick, 'High Court Approves £129m fine for Tesco Over Accounting Scandal', *The Guardian* (April 10, 2017).

[126] Ashley Armstrong, 'Tesco Fraud Trail Adjourned as Serious Fraud Office Braces for Change', *The Telegraph* (September 4, 2017).

[127] SFO, 'Press Release, SFO Agrees Deferred Prosecution with Tesco' (April 10, 2017).

[128] Theft Act 1968, s.17.

[129] Fraud Act 2006, s.1 and 4.

5 DEFERRED PROSECUTION AGREEMENTS: IN PRACTICE   113

started in September 2017, and, at the time of writing (January 2018), had not been concluded.[130]

Official details of the underlying fraudulent behaviour as well as the terms of the DPA or corresponding statement of facts have not yet been made publicly available due to the on-going trial. However, in terms of the total financial costs to Tesco Plc, these amounted to £235 million. This included £129 million in financial penalties as part of the DPA terms, the expected costs of an FCA compensation scheme of £85 million,[131] and related legal costs.[132]

Key Issues in the Tesco Case

As with the previous three DPAs, the centrality of cooperation to a corporate's ability to negotiate a DPA is reinforced by both the regulator and the regulated. As Tesco stated:

> Over the last two and a half years, Tesco PLC has fully cooperated with the investigation and undertaken an extensive programme of change, which the SFO has recognised in offering the DPA. This programme includes extensive changes to leadership, structures, financial controls, partnerships with suppliers, and the way the business buys and sells.[133]

---

[130] After this book had been submitted to the publisher, the trial was abandoned when one of the defendants suffered a heart attack. The SFO announced that they will face a re-trial. See Jane Croft, 'Former Tesco executives to face re-trial over accounting scandal', *Financial Times* (March 2, 2018).

[131] This relates to a finding of market abuse by the FCA with respect to a Tesco trading statement announced in August 2014. This statement overstated the expected profits of the Group at that time and arose from the same 'historic accounting practices' as relating to the DPA. In terms of the compensation scheme, Tesco agreed to compensate certain net purchasers of Tesco ordinary shares and listed bonds who purchased those securities for cash between 29 August 2014 and 19 September 2014. For further details see FCA Press Release, 'Tesco to pay redress for market abuse' (March 23, 2017).

[132] Roger Best, 'Serious Fraud Office Concludes Deferred Prosecution Agreement with Tesco Stores Limited', Clifford Chance—Briefing Note (April 2017), available at: https://www.cliffordchance.com/briefings/2017/04/serious_fraud_officeconcludesdeferre.html (last accessed January 30, 2018).

[133] Tesco Plc, Press Release—Deferred Prosecution Agreement in Relation to Historic Accounting Practices (March 28, 2017).

Structural and cultural reform, in addition to improved internal compliance also again form part of the narrative. Thus, we see shared beliefs around the expectations of DPAs reinforced in the public discourse, and the legitimation of the mechanism through the action and engagement of major corporate players, such as Tesco, with the enforcement authority. An OECD report in 2017 into the UK's implementation of its Anti-Bribery Convention 1998 indicated that the Southwark Crown Court judges they visited 'considered that the construction of DPAs in the UK has been quite robust and proportionate' with 'appropriate checks and balances' for the courts.[134] However, it was also pointed out that DPAs have 'no focus on the responsibility of individuals, which justices would normally focus on'.[135] Notable in the case of Tesco is the pursuit of individual prosecutions. This prosecution of individual wrongdoers is the first such prosecution related to a DPA negotiated with the SFO—though there remains the possibility of prosecutions being brought against individuals in both the Rolls Royce and XYZ Ltd DPAs. Ensuring Directors are accountable and individually liable ought to be a fundamental consideration in any DPA. In terms of social fairness and procedural justice, criminal behaviours occurring over time should receive equal treatment.

Conclusion

DPAs are located within the criminal law framework and this is important for purposes of moral retribution and perceived social fairness, justice and legitimacy. The symbolic and (potentially) deterrent nature (though empirical data here is lacking) of the criminal law enables the state (i) to negotiate regulation with corporates through the underlying threat of prosecution (corporates cannot be sure that prosecution is unlikely) and in doing so (ii) demonstrate to the various publics that it is actively responding to corporate economic crimes. In this sense, DPAs may enable the SFO to reinforce its prosecutorial role while accomplishing 'justice' through negotiation and persuasion which fits in with ideological and political agendas. However, there remain some concerns both as to the appropriateness of using DPAs rather than full criminal

---

[134] OECD, *Implementing the OECD Anti-Bribery Convention. Phase 4 Report: United Kingdom* (OECD, 2017), p. 56.
[135] Ibid.

prosecution and as to whether corporates are treated differently (when compared to individuals who engage in crime).

The DPA regime is, of course, underpinned by a sound legal foundation, thus the SFO, as primary enforcer, has at a normative level validly acquired the power to negotiate justice through deferred prosecution. But, given the small number of cases so far and the issues of concern raised, it is yet to be seen whether these powers are being properly (and 'fairly') exercised. Furthermore, there are mixed messages as regards the extent to which the underlying values and standards of the DPA regime and its rules are accepted across the regulated community. For instance, while some corporates, such as Standard Bank, have engaged with the process and thus legitimated the state's use of DPAs, others such as Rolls Royce were not initially proactive or forthcoming in their engagement. This raises some important empirical questions in relation to the perception, beliefs and actions of business towards DPAs. The many key issues that have arisen in the DPAs entered into to date demonstrate that this area of enforcement is continually evolving; we must wait for future DPAs to shed further light on the DPA jurisprudence.

CHAPTER 6

Calling to Answer?

Abstract This final chapter reinforces our contention that corporate crime *is* crime and ought to be dealt with as such. The reality, however, is that this is not the case; indeed, corporate prosecutions (particularly involving larger corporates) are relatively rare. Part of the problem here is the inadequacy of corporate criminal liability laws in the UK. This chapter argues that a criminal law-focused approach serves an important communicative function—calling wrongdoers to account as well as expressing societal condemnation of the activity in question.

Keywords Corporate criminal liability · Identification principle · Controlling mind · Monetary sanction · Corporate sanctions · Criminal law · Accountability

Corporate crime *is* crime. That is self-evident. But for *criminal* justice to be accomplished, and for associated enforcement to be seen as legitimate, just and fair, corporate crime ought to be dealt with through corresponding criminal law sanctioning mechanisms. This statement might appear relatively straightforward, but the reality of responding to corporate crime is anything but straightforward—particularly when we see the social and political downgrading of these behaviours, through state decisions instead to pursue *regulatory* and/or *civil* justice. But does regulatory and/or civil justice represent justice in cases of corporate crime?

© The Author(s) 2018
C. King and N. Lord, *Negotiated Justice and Corporate Crime*, Crime Prevention and Security Management,
https://doi.org/10.1007/978-3-319-78562-2_6

Do such responses simply *accommodate* corporate crime? Given the multifarious economic pressures (i.e. resource starvation, or abundance in response to less harmful but more direct crimes), or normative and ideological preferences of the executive, can such responses still be considered 'legitimate', both on a normative and an empirical level? These are questions that have underpinned our discussion in this book.

We ask these questions as, when corporates commit crime, UK prosecutors have traditionally been faced with the binary options—prosecute or do not prosecute. Today, however, there are other options outside the traditional criminal law route. Civil recovery is one example, whereby enforcement agencies can target property deriving from criminal activity—even without the requirement of criminal conviction. More recently, and already even more prominent, there are deferred prosecution agreements (DPAs) whereby no criminal prosecution will be brought in exchange for the corporate fulfilling certain requirements. These non-prosecution options are now central tools in responding to wrongdoing by major corporate players, with the emphasis on negotiation and accommodation, rather than prosecution and punishment. A trajectory is emerging in the UK response to corporate crimes that sees the criminal status of these actions as more dependent on the nature of the negotiated relationship between regulators and regulatees, rather than on the inherent 'social bads' that represent the basis on which these harmful behaviours were criminalised. Thus, while we contend that corporate crime *is* crime, and ought to be regarded as such, that stance is not reflected in criminal justice responses from the state.

Part of the problem in this regard is the inadequacy of corporate criminal liability laws in the UK, which has inevitably led to the emergence of alternative ways to deal with serious corporate crimes. The prosecutorial difficulties relating to the restrictive corporate criminal liability framework in the UK have been recognised by the government.[1] The inadequacy of corporate criminal liability laws, accompanied by difficulties in obtaining (admissible) evidence, has resulted in prosecutions of corporates for serious criminal offences being a rare sight in the UK,[2]

---

[1] See, for example, Ministry of Justice, *Corporate Liability for Economic Crime, Call for Evidence*. Cm 9370 (January 2017).

[2] There are, of course, notable exceptions, though these are primarily small companies, rather than the larger global corporations at the centre of recent scandals. Examples include F.H. Bertling Ltd (SFO, 'Press Release—SFO Secures Seven Convictions in $20m F.H. Bertling Corruption Case' (September 26, 2017)) and Smith and Ouzman

particularly in relation to large corporates. Other reasons, in the context of specific criminal offences, include executive interference to prevent criminal prosecution.[3] That is the context against which we see greater emphasis on non-prosecution routes to tackle corporate wrongdoing, or to put it another way greater focus on negotiated settlements. As Wells notes, there is now a move in the direction of classic regulatory techniques of negotiation and settlement.[4]

KEY ISSUES IN (UK) CORPORATE CRIMINAL LIABILITY

As Maurice Punch neatly stated, the criminal law has never quite adapted to dealing with corporates, it struggles to deal with complex multinationals with subsidiaries in different jurisdictions, and this remains so 'despite the fact that jurisprudence in Britain has for more than a century recognized that an organisation can be held to have committed a criminal act'.[5] Historically, there was significant judicial reluctance and procedural obstacles to the imposition of criminal liability on corporates.[6] Today, however, it is well established that a corporate can be held criminally liable—though there are significant practical and political difficulties with doing so.

(SFO, 'Press Release—Convicted Printing Company Sentenced and Ordered to Pay £2.2 Million (January 8, 2016)). For further discussion of the challenges involved, see Laureen Snider and Steven Bittle, 'The Challenge of Regulating Powerful Economic Actors', in James Gobert and Ana-Maria Pascal (eds), *European Developments in Corporate Criminal Liability* (Routledge, 2011).

[3] For example, the investigation into corruption by BAE Systems was halted on the grounds of security interests: see David Leigh and Rob Evans, "'National Interest' Halts Arms Corruption Inquiry', *The Guardian* (December 15, 2008). That interference was subsequently criticised: see Ben Russell and Nigel Morris, 'Court Condemns Blair for Halting Saudi Arms Inquiry', *The Independent* (April 10, 2008).

[4] Celia Wells, 'Containing Corporate Crime: Civil or Criminal Controls?', in James Gobert and Ana-Maria Pascal (eds), *European Developments in Corporate Criminal Liability* (Routledge, 2011).

[5] Maurice Punch, 'The Organizational Component in Corporate Crime', in James Gobert and Ana-Maria Pascal (eds), *European Developments in Corporate Criminal Liability* (Routledge, 2011), p. 102.

[6] For an excellent discussion of the historical development of corporate criminal liability, see Amanda Pinto and Martin Evans, *Corporate Criminal Liability* (3rd ed, Sweet and Maxwell, 2013), particularly ch. 2; Celia Wells, *Corporations and Criminal Responsibility* (2nd ed, Oxford University Press, 2001), ch. 5.

Perhaps most notable here is the identification principle, which requires that the natural person who commits the *actus reus* of an offence must be identified with the corporate.[7] In effect, this approach restricts corporate criminal liability to those cases where a senior official, or what is referred to as the 'controlling mind', is involved in the criminal wrong. Such a narrow approach makes it difficult to prosecute large corporates (as opposed to smaller ones), given that in such corporates the board of directors will be removed from the coalface. As Pinto and Evans state:

> The prosecution of larger corporations is difficult despite their having greater power to harm. A conviction for a general, as opposed to a regulatory, offence is only likely where the corporation is very small, such as a one-man band or family business, because in this type of case, if an offence has been committed within the company, it is likely to have been committed by the director or other senior officer. Paradoxically this is the sort of case in which a separate prosecution of the company would serve no practical purpose. In the case of a substantial corporation, a director will seldom have sufficient proximity to the unlawful act to be personally liable and without such personal liability on the part of a person who is the directing mind and will of the corporation, liability cannot be attributed to it. The impact of the doctrine of identification has been to limit general criminal liability for practical purposes to those entities at the very bottom of the corporate scale.[8]

As we saw in Chapter 2, equal treatment before the law is fundamental to ensuring procedural justice, and therefore the legitimacy of enforcement, for regulated communities. The legacy of differential treatment of corporates of different sizes raises important questions about how legitimate the enforcement can be said to be. For instance, it can be expected that there will be an absence of moral condemnation through the standard criminal law route for large corporates, giving rise to concern as to

---

[7]The leading case is *Tesco Supermarkets Ltd v Nattrass* [1972] AC 153. The identification principle will be applied to determine corporate criminal liability when no test is set out in the relevant statute. See, for example, Corporate Manslaughter and Corporate Homicide Act 2007, s.1; Bribery Act 2010, s.1. For further discussion, see James Gobert, 'Country Report: UK', in James Gobert and Ana-Maria Pascal (eds), *European Developments in Corporate Criminal Liability* (Routledge, 2011), pp. 317–319.

[8]Amanda Pinto and Martin Evans, *Corporate Criminal Liability* (3rd ed, Sweet and Maxwell, 2013), p. 50.

different *standards* of justice.[9] This has important implications for the pursuit of legitimacy as the available or likely enforcement responses are determined by factors outside of the nature of the criminal behaviour. As Punch points out, the identification principle 'virtually grants immunity to large companies against conviction',[10] while Clarkson notes how it does not reflect modern corporate practice—particularly in larger corporates.[11] While it is now established that a corporate can be held criminally liable, corporate criminal liability remains contentious. The underlying assumption in the narrative above is that corporations should be liable to criminal prosecution when they knowingly engage in criminal behaviour but some argue that the criminal law is not suitable in these scenarios.[12] Against this backdrop, the following sub-sections (i) consider criticisms of corporate criminal liability and (ii) argue that corporates can (and should) be held criminally liable for their crimes.

Criticisms of Corporate Criminal Liability: An Overview

It is our contention that there is value in criminally prosecuting corporates who commit criminal activity. Whilst recognising difficulties in criminal enforcement, our view is that corporate criminal liability does have an important and purposeful role to play in communicating wrong, holding wrongdoers accountable, and expressing societal condemnation of the wrongdoing in question. As Durkheim argued, the nature

---

[9] See Louise Dunford and Ann Ridley, '"No Soul to Be Damned, No Body to Be Kicked": Responsibility, Blame and Corporate Punishment', *International Journal of the Sociology of Law* (1996), 24: 1.

[10] Maurice Punch, 'The Organizational Component in Corporate Crime', in James Gobert and Ana-Maria Pascal (eds), *European Developments in Corporate Criminal Liability* (Routledge, 2011), p. 110.

[11] C.M.V. Clarkson, 'Kicking Corporate Bodies and Damning Their Souls', *Modern Law Review* (1996), 59: 557, 561.

[12] In recent years, new (criminal law) approaches to tackling corporate crime have been introduced, including various 'failure to prevent' offences. For further discussion see, for example, Celia Wells, 'Corporate Failure to Prevent Economic Crime—a Proposal', *Criminal Law Review* (2017): 426. Alongside such 'failure' offences, there are also non-prosecution responses—as discussed in this book. One issue that arises here is whether non-prosecution routes can continue to be justified (as responses to inadequacies in the criminal law) when the evolving criminal law is, arguably, equipped to target corporates. We thank Dr. John Child for this point.

of punishment inheres emotional, communicative and moral aspects, and is in these ways functional (though we must ask for whom).[13] Not everyone subscribes to this view, however. Indeed, Khanna argues that while '[c]orporate criminal liability is an institution of considerable antiquity...there is little understanding of what, if anything, it is designed to achieve'.[14]

Many scholars argue that criminal liability should not attach to corporates. For example, Alschuler contends that corporate criminal liability punishes the innocent, and that such punishment of innocent shareholders and employees ought not be regarded as a secondary consequence.[15] It is due to such collateral effects that Khanna promotes modified forms of corporate *civil* liability, particularly as civil liability can capture the desirable features of corporate criminal liability, such as powerful enforcement responses usually attached to public enforcement, and extensive prelitigation information gathering.[16] Furthermore, Hasnas contends that there is no theoretical justification for corporate criminal liability; he argues that assigning criminal responsibility to corporate entities violates the theoretical structure of Anglo-American criminal law.[17]

It has also been suggested that 'criminal punishment cannot really be borne by a fictional entity'.[18] Indeed, a sentence often uttered in this context is: 'Did you ever expect a corporation to have a conscience

---

[13] Emile Durkheim, *The Division of Labour in Society* (The Free Press, 1997). See also Peter Henning, 'Should the Perception of Corporate Punishment Matter?', *Journal of Law and Policy* (2010), 19(1): 83, 93.

[14] Vikramaditya S. Khanna, 'Corporate Criminal Liability: What Purpose Does It Serve?', *Harvard Law Review* (1996), 109(7): 1477, 1532.

[15] Albert W. Alschuler, 'Two Ways to Think About the Punishment of Corporations', *American Criminal Law Review* (2009), 46: 1359. He does acknowledge though that—much to his regret—corporate criminal liability is here to stay.

[16] Vikramaditya S. Khanna, 'Corporate Criminal Liability: What Purpose Does It Serve?', *Harvard Law Review* (1996), 109(7): 1477, 1532.

[17] John Hasnas, 'The Centenary of a Mistake: One Hundred Years of Corporate Criminal Liability', *American Criminal Law Review* (2009), 46: 1329. See also John Hasnas, 'Where Is Flex Cohen When We Need Him: Transcendental Nonsense and the Moral Responsibility of Corporations', *Journal of Law and Policy* (2010), 19: 55.

[18] Albert W. Alschuler, 'Two Ways to Think About the Punishment of Corporations', *American Criminal Law Review* (2009), 46: 1359, 1367.

when it has no soul to be damned and no body to be kicked'.[19] Baker argues that

> Corporations neither deserve nor attract our sympathy. Sympathy involves the capacity for sharing or understanding the feelings or interests of others. Modern corporations are abstract, impersonal, utilitarian entities lacking emotions and a personal story, and as such they do not deserve sympathy simply because they are not human. For that reason alone, they should not be the subjects of criminal prosecution.[20]

Baker goes on to state: 'Whatever theory or approach one adopts to justify corporate criminal liability, one cannot escape from the reality that corporations are being punished without regard for culpability. To say that a corporation is "at fault" for the acts or omissions of its officers, directors, or employees dispenses with mens rea'.[21] In light of such criticisms, it is worthwhile considering whether corporates can be held criminally liable (the answer is, of course, 'yes') before turning to examining the value of corporate criminal liability.

Can Corporates Be Held Criminally Liable?

Before turning to consider the value of corporate criminal liability, it is important to consider the deceptively simple question: can corporates be held criminally liable? In our view, this should be answered in the affirmative. Exploring this further, we contend that corporates—legal persons—are suitable and appropriate subjects for the criminal law. Moreover, we argue that the criminal law is a necessary, indeed desirable, approach to dealing with corporate wrongdoers.

First, are corporates suitable subjects for the criminal law? Or, to look at this another way, who should be held criminally liable when crimes take place by, within, or facilitated by a corporate in the course of business. Should it be the *individual* (i.e. the person (i) that commits the actual act

---

[19] This phrase was uttered by Baron Thurlow, as quoted by Amanda Pinto and Martin Evans, *Corporate Criminal Liability* (3rd ed, Sweet and Maxwell, 2013), p. 14, referring to Poynder, *Literary Extracts* (1844), vol. 1.

[20] John S. Baker Jr, 'Reforming Corporations Through Threats of Federal Prosecution', *Cornell Law Review* (2004), 89(2): 310, 350.

[21] Ibid.

(or omission) or (ii) whose policies lead to and facilitate such behaviours) or the *company* (whose existence provides the opportunity and environment for the crime)? Such questions invoke debates over whether corporates are reducible to their individuals or whether a corporate can represent more than the sum of its individuals.[22] It also invokes philosophical deliberation over whether criminal liability requires moral blameworthiness or a moral conscience, an emotional capacity that corporations cannot possess.[23] Of course, corporates are constellations of individuals but the fundamental question is when do such configurations of people become more than, and thus separate to, the sum of their parts? Ultimately—and while some argue that the focus should be on 'flesh and blood' persons, whereas others contend that the focus should be solely on the corporate, as a rational unitary actor[24]—for the purposes of this book we do not engage further with such issues, simply because UK law allows both 'flesh and blood' persons *and* corporations to be criminally prosecuted.[25]

In relation to corporate criminal liability, three facets must be mentioned: corporate 'personality', 'responsibility' and 'culture'.[26] In law, corporates can be attributed the same rights and responsibilities as natural persons and, in essence, are afforded a corporate *personality*. As a personality, a corporate can have *responsibility*.[27] The nature of the

---

[22] James Gobert and Maurice Punch, *Rethinking Corporate Crime* (Butterworths, 2003), p. 49; Celia Wells, 'Corporate Crime: Opening the Eyes of the Sentry', *Legal Studies* (2010), 30(3): 370.

[23] Ana-Maria Pascal, 'A Legal Person's Conscience: Philosophical Underpinnings of Corporate Criminal Liability', in James Gobert and Ana-Maria Pascal (eds), *European Developments in Corporate Criminal Liability* (Routledge, 2011).

[24] For further discussion, see Jennifer Hill, 'Corporate Criminal Liability in Australia: An Evolving Corporate Governance Technique?', *Journal of Business Law* (2003): 1, 7 *et seq.*

[25] It has been suggested that to optimally deter corporate crime, both individual and corporate criminal liability should be imposed by the state: see Jennifer Arlen, 'Corporate Criminal Liability: Theory and Evidence', in Alan Harel and Keith N. Hylton (eds), *Research Handbook on the Economics of Criminal Law* (Edward Elgar, 2012).

[26] We deliberately do not engage with these facets in detail; for more in-depth discussion see Celia Wells, 'Corporate Crime: Opening the Eyes of the Sentry', *Legal Studies* (2010), 30(3): 370, 379–383.

[27] 'If legal personification entailed the ability to possess inherent rights, it also carried with it the capacity to bear duties. Indeed, it has been argued that the debate on corporate personality for the purposes of determining rights of corporations is now obsolete and the new challenge and focus of debate for contemporary industrialised societies is to ensure corporate responsibility and accountability'. Jennifer Hill, 'Corporate Criminal Liability

personality and responsibility is shaped and driven by the organisational *culture*. As Punch notes, a 'firm's institutional context and culture shape an environment that encourages, colludes or is culpably blind to law-breaking'.[28] Thus, the 'corporate person' is in many ways distinct from its individuals and so the corporate itself can bear responsibility and liability, making it suitable for criminal law interventions.[29]

Next we must ask: are criminal law responses desirable and necessary? This question is central to our thesis that, as a matter of justice, criminal enforcement against corporate crime is desired; where a corporate commits a crime then that corporate should be held accountable for its actions and exposed to societal condemnation.[30] For example, in the context of the Gulf of Mexico oil spill, Uhlmann has argued that '[c]riminal prosecution will deter future spills more than civil penalties alone ... will ensure restitution to victims of the Gulf oil spill ... [and] will express societal condemnation of the conduct that caused the Gulf oil spill in ways that civil enforcement cannot'.[31] This is only a viable argument, however, if the regulated community perceives that a large enough proportion of all cases of criminality are detected and then prosecuted. A perceived certainty of detection and certainty of prosecution are key conditions for the criminal law to act as a deterrent to those who might drift into or seek to commit crimes. Thus, alongside considerations of criminal enforcement, it is important to also consider levels of resources made available to authorities (this point is picked up again later on).

Some scholars have argued instead for the pursuit of civil corporate sanctions and/or the liability of individual managers and directors. Such

in Australia: An Evolving Corporate Governance Technique?', *Journal of Business Law* (2003): 1, 6–7.

[28] Maurice Punch, 'The Organizational Component in Corporate Crime', in James Gobert and Ana-Maria Pascal (eds), *European Developments in Corporate Criminal Liability* (Routledge, 2011), p. 101.

[29] However, the creation of the corporate personality can dehumanise and depersonalise the corporation from its individuals, creating scope for 'structured irresponsibility' Steve Tombs and David Whyte, *The Corporate Criminal: Why Corporations Must Be Abolished* (Routledge, 2015), p. 100.

[30] See also William S. Laufer, *Corporate Bodies and Guilty Minds: The Failure of Corporate Criminal Liability* (University of Chicago Press, 2006).

[31] David M. Uhlmann, 'After the Spill Is Gone: The Gulf of Mexico, Environmental Crime, and the Criminal Law', *Michigan Law Review* (2011), 109: 1413, 1419.

arguments are based on the premise that state costs are lowered, that the evidential burden is lessened, and that damages awarded better reflect victims' losses and therefore achieve 'justice' if this is best served in terms of financial compensation.[32] However, these arguments do not stand up to scrutiny. Civil sanctions supposedly encourage companies to invest more in prevention to avoid financial penalties but this provides insufficient deterrence as the purported amoral nature of corporate decision-making results not in investment in prevention but preparation for possible damages that over time are lower. Moreover, what of cases where, for example, the cost of prevention is higher than damages likely to be awarded in civil proceedings?[33] Or, if a company decides that it is not in its financial interest to spend significant amounts on safety/prevention, when it might only be liable for much smaller amounts if subsequently sued for damages. There are further difficulties in relying upon civil sanctions to deter corporate crime. For example, identifiable victims and plaintiffs able and willing to bring lawsuits are often lacking or non-existent, victims may not even be aware of victim status or may not know against whom to litigate. Persistent recidivism cannot be considered and reform cannot be compelled (allowing corporations to posit that their 'way of doing business' is not illegal) and the reputational threat associated with criminal sanctioning is circumvented.[34] Ultimately, we subscribe to the view that 'civil suits are not an adequate substitute for criminal prosecutions' in the context of corporate crimes.[35] Our view is that a criminal law response to corporate crime is more appropriate than civil sanctions,[36]

---

[32] See, for example, Vikramaditya S. Khanna, 'Corporate Crime Legislation: A Political Economy Analysis', *Washington University Law Quarterly* (2004), 82: 95; Vikramaditya S. Khanna, 'Corporate Criminal Liability: What Purpose Does It Serve?', *Harvard Law Review* (1996), 109(7): 1477.

[33] For discussion in the context of the Ford Pinto case, see Francis T. Cullen, Gray Cavender, William J. Maakestad, and Michael L. Benson, *Corporate Crime Under Attack: The Fight to Criminalize Business Violence* (2nd ed, Routledge, 2015).

[34] For further discussion, see James Gobert and Maurice Punch, *Rethinking Corporate Crime* (Butterworths, 2003), pp. 50–53.

[35] James Gobert and Maurice Punch, *Rethinking Corporate Crime* (Butterworths, 2003), p. 53.

[36] The issue of 'appropriateness' is different to considerations of 'effectiveness' (for example, whether criminal or civil sanctions are more effective). For further discussion see Michael Watson, 'The Enforcement of Environmental Law: Civil or Criminal Penalties?', *Environmental Law and Management* (2005), 17(1): 3; Andrew B. Miller, 'What Makes

not least in that criminal prosecution and conviction results in the corporate being labelled *criminal* and being punished accordingly. In other words, the corporate criminal is held accountable for its crime—which we turn to in the next section.

THE COMMUNICATIVE VALUE OF CORPORATE CRIMINAL LIABILITY

Corporate criminal liability does, we suggest, serve an important function, namely in communicating wrong, holding wrongdoers accountable, and expressing societal condemnation for the activity in question. As Duff et al. suggest,

> a plausible normative theory of the criminal law will not portray it simply as an attempt to establish the truth as to whether the defendant committed the offence charged, in order to identify accurately those who are to be subjected to punishment. It will instead portray it as a process through which a citizen is called to answer a charge of criminal wrongdoing. A conception of, and search for, the truth is still central to that portrayal: an essential aim of the trial is to establish whether the charge of wrongdoing is proved to be true. However, first, the truth that is to be established is a normative truth about the defendant's alleged wrongdoing – and if what is established is the normative truth that she is guilty of that wrongdoing, its declaration by the fact-finder is also a condemnation of the defendant.[37]

Companies Behave? An Analysis of Criminal and Civil Penalties Under Environmental Law' (December 2005), available at: https://papers.ssrn.com/sol3/papers.cfm?abstract_id=471841 (last accessed January 28, 2018); Kenneth G. Dau-Schmidt, 'An Economic Analysis of the Criminal Law as a Preference-Shaping Policy', *Duke Law Journal* (1990), 1; Brent Fisse and John Braithwaite, 'The Allocation of Responsibility for Corporate Crime: Individualism, Collectivism and Accountability', *Sydney Law Review* (1988), 11: 468, 493. In the UK, the use of civil sanctions has expanded following the Hampton and Macrory reports: Philip Hampton, *Reducing administrative burdens: effective inspection and enforcement* (March 2005); Richard B. Macrory, *Regulatory Justice: Making Sanctions Effective—Final Report* (November 2006).

[37] See Anthony Duff, Lindsay Farmer, Sandra Marshall, and Victor Tadros, *The Trial on Trial, Vol. 3: Towards a Normative Theory of the Criminal Trial* (Hart, 2007), p. 119. For a critique, see Abenaa Owusu-Bempah, *Defendant Participation in the Criminal Process* (Routledge, 2017), pp. 51–59.

In the context of corporate wrongdoing, Wells has suggested that: 'The public nature of criminal prosecutions plays an important role in conveying cultural messages about types of behaviour and offences'.[38] As Uhlmann notes, 'criminal prosecution will express societal condemnation of the conduct ... in ways that civil enforcement cannot, which is one of the purposes of the criminal law'.[39] He goes on to state that if a criminal prosecution were not brought 'the government would send the wrong message about the ecological damage to the Gulf, the suffering of the communities along the Gulf coast, and the value of the lives of the workers who died when the Deepwater Horizon exploded'.[40]

Moreover, corporate crime invariably will be a matter of public concern.[41] This aspect of criminal law is recognised by those who criticise corporate criminal liability laws: for example, Hasnas notes the requirement that 'criminal sanction be applied only to address harm to a societal rather than private interest, and then only when its use is necessary to protect that interest'.[42] He suggests, however, that corporate criminal liability laws do not satisfy these requirements. We disagree in this regard; our view is that corporate crime is concerned with public/societal interests[43] and that those interests ought to be protected by criminal sanction. Our view is that the criminal law is an appropriate tool to hold wrongdoers accountable.

---

[38] Celia Wells, *Corporations and Criminal Responsibility* (2nd ed, Oxford University Press, 2001), p. 30. For consideration of re-integrative shaming, see John Braithwaite, *Crime, Shame and Reintegration* (Cambridge University Press, 1989). See also John Braithwaite and Peter Drahos, 'Zero Tolerance, Naming and Shaming: Is There a Case for It with Crimes of the Powerful?', *Australian and New Zealand Journal of Criminology* (2002), 35(3): 269. For discussion of 'reputation-orientated sanctions', see James Gobert and Maurice Punch, *Rethinking Corporate Crime* (Butterworths, 2003), pp. 236–239.

[39] David M. Uhlmann, 'After the Spill Is Gone: The Gulf of Mexico, Environmental Crime, and the Criminal Law', *Michigan Law Review* (2011), 109: 1413, 1419.

[40] Ibid.

[41] See James Fitzjames Stephen, *A History of the Criminal Law of England, Vol. II* (William S. Hein, reprint: 1883), 76.

[42] John Hasnas, 'The Centenary of a Mistake: One Hundred Years of Corporate Criminal Liability', *American Criminal Law Review* (2009), 46: 1329, 1345.

[43] The recent financial crisis is just one example of where corporate 'misconduct' has adversely affected public/societal interests.

Duff et al. suggest that the commission of public wrongs must be answered for[44] and identify four aspects of such holding to account:

> First, it is a way of taking wrongdoing seriously, as wrongdoing. ... Second, such calling to account is also a way of taking the wrongdoers seriously, and of treating them with the respect that is due to them as responsible agents. ... Third, to call a person to account for her wrongdoing in this way involves an attempt (or an aspiration) to persuade her to accept the judgment that she did wrong, and to make it her own – to accept and make her own not just the bare judgment *that* she committed a wrong, but the understanding of the character and seriousness of the wrong that the process of calling her to account should express. ... Fourth, such calling to account requires a shared language in which the accuser can call and the accused can answer, a language that expresses the (supposedly) shared values and understandings in terms of which the wrongs can be identified and characterised, and responsibility and liability for them can be argued and ascribed.[45]

Corporate wrongdoing invariably causes harm, for which the corporate ought to be held to account. While there may be justification in trying to avert wrongdoing in advance or in appropriate responses to the victims of wrongdoing, it is also important to 'recognise the doing, as well as the suffering, of wrong, by seeking to call the doer to account'.[46] Our stance is that that the criminal law is an appropriate venue for such calling to account. Criminal prosecution clearly conveys that the actions in question were wrong and merit punishment, furthering the communicative aim with the (corporate) wrongdoer fully involved in the process of judgment.

One particular complaint levied against corporate criminal liability laws must be considered further, namely that regardless of whether civil or criminal proceedings are pursued, the punishment (assuming

---

[44] They note that 'wrongs are "public" in this sense if they are wrongs for which we must answer to our fellow citizens (as distinct from merely private wrongs for which we must answer only to some other and smaller community)'. Anthony Duff, Lindsay Farmer, Sandra Marshall, and Victor Tadros, *The Trial on Trial, Vol. 3: Towards a Normative Theory of the Criminal Trial* (Hart, 2007), p. 137.

[45] Ibid., p. 137 *et seq.*

[46] Ibid.

successful proceedings) tends to be in the form of a monetary fine.[47] Thus, why go to the bother of criminal trial? Hasnas goes further and states that, where a financial sanction is imposed on a company, it will be the owners (shareholders) who incur the penalty.[48] He suggests that this result leads to punishment of the innocent, which cannot further the legitimate aims of punishment.[49] There are two points to emphasise here: first, granted that there is no prospect of incarceration for a corporate offender, there is nonetheless value in pursuing criminal proceedings.[50] We repeat our earlier point that there is value in holding a corporate accountable for its crime (or crime committed on its behalf). As Duff et al. say, 'It makes sense … to try to call wrongdoers to account even if nothing is to be done to or about them beyond that process of calling to account'.[51] Or, as Clarkson states, 'If it is the company that is culpable, then it is the company that deserves prosecution and punishment'.[52] It is the corporate itself that is fined (not the owners/shareholders), and it is the corporate that should be saddled with any stigma that arises from criminal conviction.

Second, the suggestion that it is innocent owners/shareholders who will suffer has been criticised: 'What this account misses is the reality that corporations are not fictions. Rather, they are enormously powerful, and very real, actors whose conduct often causes very significant harm both to individuals and to society as a whole'.[53]

---

[47] See Criminal Justice Act 2003, s.163. For consideration of sentencing of corporate defendants, see Amanda Pinto and Martin Evans, *Corporate Criminal Liability* (3rd ed, Sweet and Maxwell, 2013), ch. 10.

[48] Unless, as Hasnas notes, that penalty can be passed on to consumers.

[49] John Hasnas, 'The Centenary of a Mistake: One Hundred Years of Corporate Criminal Liability', *American Criminal Law Review* (2009), 46: 1329, 1338–1339.

[50] A more flippant retort might be that since there is no prospect of imprisonment, then corporates should be less concerned since they cannot go to prison! See Sara Sun Beale, 'A Response to the Critics of Corporate Criminal Liability', *American Criminal Law Review* (2009), 46: 1481, 1488.

[51] Anthony Duff, Lindsay Farmer, Sandra Marshall, and Victor Tadros, *The Trial on Trial, Vol. 3: Towards a Normative Theory of the Criminal Trial* (Hart, 2007), pp. 142–143.

[52] C.M.V. Clarkson, 'Kicking Corporate Bodies and Damning Their Souls', *Modern Law Review* (1996), 59: 557, 562.

[53] Sara Sun Beale, 'A Response to the Critics of Corporate Criminal Liability', *American Criminal Law Review* (2009), 46: 1481, 1482.

Moreover, a corporate is a separate legal entity, distinct from its owners/shareholders. If a corporate is successful, then the owners/shareholders will benefit. In a similar vein, if a corporate is successfully sued (e.g. for breach of contract or for committing a tort) and the corporate is compelled to pay compensation and possibly even punitive damages, then the owners/shareholders will lose equity. What is the difference between such a civil action against the corporate and a criminal monetary punishment? It would be disingenuous to suggest that owners/shareholders should benefit from success, but not the consequences of wrongdoing on the part of the corporate.[54]

Furthermore, criticisms that innocent owners/shareholders bear the consequences of corporate criminal liability fall down at a more principled level. In criminal proceedings against a person (e.g. for murder, assault, etc.), innocent family members, for example, might be affected. If the defendant is imprisoned following conviction, family members are deprived of the company of their father/mother/son/daughter, whatever the case may be. If the defendant is the breadwinner of the family, those innocent family members are affected. If the defendant is ordered to pay a criminal fine, again innocent family members can be affected. Such considerations do not influence whether an individual ought to be criminally prosecuted for his/her wrongdoing.[55]

Moreover, the suggestion that there is no value in going after innocent shareholders has been rejected by UK authorities in the context of civil proceedings for corporate wrongdoing. For example, in Mabey Engineering (Holdings) Ltd,[56] a civil recovery order was imposed in respect of sums received through share dividends derived from contracts that had been won as a result of unlawful conduct. The then-SFO Director, Richard Alderman, was unrepentant that shareholders were confronted with civil proceedings for the unlawful conduct of a

---

[54] For further discussion see Sara Sun Beale, 'A Response to the Critics of Corporate Criminal Liability', *American Criminal Law Review* (2009), 46: 1481, 1484–1486.

[55] Though they might be considered at the sentencing stage, for example in relation to ability to pay. Of course, ability to pay could also be taken into consideration when sentencing a corporate.

[56] See the Stolen Asset Recovery Initiative (StAR) Corruption Database 'Mabey Engineering (Holdings) Ltd', available at: http://star.worldbank.org/corruption-cases/node/20233 (last accessed July 28, 2017); James Hurley, 'SFO Targets "Criminal" Companies' Dividends', *The Telegraph* (January 12, 2012).

subsidiary company.[57] So, assuming that critics of corporate criminal liability laws are not calling for corporates to get away scot-free, the suggestion that it is unfair that shareholders will be affected does not stand up.

In summary, criminal law does, we suggest, have (or, at least, ought to have) an important role to play in holding corporate wrongdoers accountable. However, it is recognised that the reality is rather different: the UK experience demonstrates that for those specialist bodies set up to regulate business, 'criminal prosecution is overwhelmingly the road not taken'.[58] According to Punch, 'This leaves one with the feeling that the criminal law and criminal justice mechanisms (enforcement, investigation, prosecution, trial and sanctions) simply do not deliver justice. The law courts are no match for powerful, devious, wealthy and unscrupulous companies, with the result that all too often the "real villains" get away with their crimes'.[59] Nowadays, there is an evident shift away from prosecuting corporate wrongdoers; instead, there is a clear preference for negotiated settlements and the accommodation of corporate wrongdoing.[60]

---

[57] He stated: *'shareholders who receive the proceeds of crime can expect civil action against them to recover the money. The SFO will pursue this approach vigorously. In this particular case, however, the shareholder was totally unaware of any inappropriate behaviour. The company and the various stakeholders across the group have worked very constructively with the SFO to resolve the situation, and we are very happy to acknowledge this. The second, broader point is that shareholders and investors in companies are obliged to satisfy themselves with the business practices of the companies they invest in. This is very important and we cannot emphasise it enough. It is particularly so for institutional investors who have the knowledge and expertise to do it. The SFO intends to use the civil recovery process to pursue investors who have benefitted from illegal activity. Where issues arise, we will be much less sympathetic to institutional investors whose due diligence has clearly been lax in this respect'.* Cited in FCPA Compliance Report, The SFO Speaks in the Mabey & Johnson Case: Private Equity—Are You Listening? available at: http://fcpacompliancereport.com/2012/01/the-sfo-speaks-in-the-mabey-johnson-case-private-equity-are-you-listening/ (last accessed January 2, 2018).

[58] Mike Levi and Nicholas Lord, 'White-Collar and Corporate Crimes', in Alison Liebling, Shadd Maruna, and Lesley McAra (eds), *Oxford Handbook of Criminology* (6th ed, Oxford University Press, 2017), p. 734.

[59] Maurice Punch, 'The Organizational Component in Corporate Crime', in James Gobert and Ana-Maria Pascal (eds), *European Developments in Corporate Criminal Liability* (Routledge, 2011), p. 111.

[60] This point is not confined to the UK; Western governments, in general, have preferred 'soft' regulation and the occasional symbolic prosecution.

CONCLUSION: WHAT LIES AHEAD?

Notwithstanding the important role of the criminal law, discussed above, there is an evident lack of appetite to prosecute complex corporate criminal offences. It has been suggested that, in terms of responding to corporate crime, the criminal justice system is difficult to use and not particularly successful.[61] The result has been that wrongdoing on the part of corporates is being 'differentially enforced'.[62] For example, in the context of corporate bribery (an offence that exemplifies the preference for negotiation and civil settlement), while UK law criminalises corporate bribery of foreign public officials,[63] prosecutions for such an offence are relatively rare. Instead, there is a clear preference on the part of enforcement authorities/regulators to negotiate with corporates.[64] In other words, there is an evident move away from 'regulation by enforcement'[65] in favour of 'regulation by settlement'.[66] This undermines perceived legitimacy as fairness before the criminal law is not consistent.

It is our view that negotiation and 'accommodation'—reflected in mechanisms such as CROs and DPAs in response to corporate crime—are now 'the normal policy response'.[67] This approach is reflective of the reality of investigating and prosecuting corporate crime, whereby law enforcement authorities are constrained by legal, procedural, evidential and, of course, financial obstacles. It is our contention that

---

[61] For an overview, see Michael L. Benson and Sally S. Simpson, *Understanding White-Collar Crime: An Opportunity Perspective* (2nd ed, Routledge, 2015), pp. 234–238.

[62] Celia Wells, 'Containing Corporate Crime. Civil or Criminal Controls?', in James Gobert and Ana-Maria Pascal (eds), *European Developments in Corporate Criminal Liability* (Routledge, 2011), p. 16. Such differential enforcement might be due to a number of factors, for example a preference for alternative (non-criminal) resolution, difficulties in bringing a successful prosecution, selection of priorities, or inadequate resources.

[63] Bribery Act 2010, s.6.

[64] Nicholas Lord and Colin King, 'Negotiating Non-Contention: Civil Recovery and Deferred Prosecution in Response to Transnational Corporate Bribery', in Liz Campbell and Nicholas Lord (eds), *Corruption in Commercial Enterprise: Law, Theory and Practice* (Routledge, 2018).

[65] Harvey L. Pitt and Karen L. Shapiro, 'Securities Regulation by Enforcement: A Look Ahead at the Next Decade', *Yale Journal on Regulation* (1990), 7: 149.

[66] Matthew C. Turk, 'Regulation by Settlement', *University of Kansas Law Review* (2017), 66: 259.

[67] Nicholas Lord, *Regulating Corporate Bribery in International Business: Anti-Corruption in the UK and Germany* (Ashgate, 2014), p. 179.

even if full resources, both financial and personnel, were available for the enforcement authorities, other antecedent factors would nonetheless lead to convergence towards accommodation. That is, there are ideological and symbolic considerations, as authorities accept that 'much corporate, economic crime requires negotiation and persuasion rather than criminal prosecution'.[68] Thus, the inadequacy of, and difficulties associated with, corporate criminal liability laws in the UK has undermined the criminal law response and has resulted in alternative approaches such as CROs and DPAs. That issue goes to the crux of our discussion throughout this book, particularly as to the legitimacy of such alternative approaches. Our starting point—that corporate crime *is* crime—has led us to argue that there is a strong normative argument in favour of using the criminal law as a primary response to corporate crime. As Garrett emphasises, 'It is crucial that we get corporate prosecutions right, given the size, seriousness, and complexity of the crimes that can occur in the corporate setting. Corporate prosecutions are themselves too big to fail'.[69]

The reality of corporate crime enforcement responses, however, reflects the differing perspectives between left idealism and left realism. In other words, corporate crime is crime and merits criminal punishment, but various factors (as discussed above) mean that the state has resorted to negotiation and accommodation to sanction such crime. Unsurprisingly, such 'negotiated justice' has attracted criticism, not least in relation to social equality, fairness and justice. In light of the foregoing, then, we conclude this book by briefly outlining some issues that will impact on future developments.

First, David Green will step down as Director of the SFO in April 2018. At the time of writing (January 2018), his successor is yet to be announced. The role of Director has been fundamental to the direction of the agency, as much discretion rests with them in dictating enforcement strategies. We see such discretion explicit in the acceptance criteria of the SFO as before taking on a case for investigation, the Director considers the following circumstances: whether the apparent criminality undermines UK PLC commercial or financial interests in

---

[68] Ibid., p. 117.
[69] Brandon L. Garrett, *Too Big to Jail: How Prosecutors Compromise with Corporations* (Harvard University Press, 2014), p. 288.

general and in the City of London in particular; whether the actual or potential financial loss involved is high; whether actual or potential economic harm is significant; whether there is a significant public interest element, and whether there is new species of fraud.[70] As David Green has regularly reiterated, the SFO is an investigator *and* prosecutor, and for the state response to serious corporate financial crimes to be legitimate, this prosecutorial function needs to remain at the forefront of the SFO's work. The future existence of the SFO as the lead authority for serious and complex frauds now appears to be certain; this is a major development for the legitimacy of the state's response to corporate financial crimes. However, there remain concerns as to sufficiency and availability of resourcing. In 2017/18, the SFO's core funding was £35.7 million.[71] For cases likely to cost more than 5% of the SFO's annual budget, so-called 'blockbuster' funding can be requested from the Treasury—the Rolls Royce case was funded in this way. This introduces an explicitly political dimension to the capabilities of the SFO.[72] There is little transparency around the decisions made in response to such requests and therefore no data on how many requests are agreed or rejected. While this may not yet have emerged as a major issue, it potentially creates tensions around the ability of the Director to operate independently of the Executive, particularly with those cases that have significant political aspects.[73] This necessary independence has been further jeopardised as the UK Government announced plans in 2017 to establish the National Economic Crime Centre (NECC). This would enable the National Crime Agency to 'directly task the Serious

---

[70] SFO, 'Guidance, Policy and Protocols', available at: https://www.sfo.gov.uk/publications/guidance-policy-and-protocols/ (last accessed January 31, 2018).

[71] Details of the SFO's funding arrangements are available on the SFO website: SFO, 'About Us', available at: https://www.sfo.gov.uk/about-us/ (last accessed January 31, 2018).

[72] A further political issue is the UK's exit from the European Union, which might create circumstances that in turn influence the extent of corporate prosecutions. As the UK government seeks to encourage business expansion outside of the EU region, in particular in regions that may be more culturally tolerant of bribery, for example, they be (even) less supportive of pursuing implicated UK corporates if to do so might jeopardise trading relations. Although such social change is likely to be significant, we do not address it explicitly in this book.

[73] The BAE Systems scandal is a case in point, as political and economic relations between the UK and Saudi Arabia were supposedly jeopardised.

Fraud Office (SFO) to investigate the worst offenders. The SFO will continue to act as an independent organisation, supporting the multi-agency response led by the NCA'.[74] However, this raises concerns that the SFO's primary focus on high-end serious and complex corporate frauds risks being undermined by the NCA's more dominant remit around organised crime and terrorism. A shift towards pursuing the 'usual suspects', rather than white-collar and corporate criminals, would move enforcement attention away from what we consider frequent, severe and harmful behaviours by otherwise respectable actors in society.

Second, what role will (or should) the criminal law play in responding to corporate crime? Those who work in this area will not be surprised to hear that traditional criminal law plays only a small role in controlling corporate illegality.[75] As Gobert and Punch stated in 2003,

> Typically, companies are prosecuted for violation of regulatory offences carrying relatively minor monetary penalties that bear little relationship to the harm that may have occurred. Even when a formal criminal prosecution is undertaken, corporate defendants are well-positioned to defend themselves. Large companies are able to hire the best lawyers, secure "professional" expert witnesses, and engage in delaying tactics that will outlast the political pressure that prompted the government to initiate a prosecution in the first place. Given the difficulties in securing a conviction, the tendency is for the parties to engage in a form of "plea-bargaining" where the company agrees to try to do better in the future and the government agrees not to prosecute for offences committed in the past.[76]

Fifteen years on, this statement still holds true. That notwithstanding, the criminal law has bared its teeth with the threat of prosecution for 'failure to prevent' offences. Such offences—for example, failure to

---

[74] HM Government Press Release, 'Home Secretary Announces New National Economic Crime Centre to Tackle High Level Fraud and Money Laundering' (December 11, 2017).

[75] James Gobert and Maurice Punch, *Rethinking Corporate Crime* (Butterworths, 2003), p. 9. Full enforcement of the criminal law has long been recognised to be idealistic, with discretionary practices central to various stages of policing. See Joseph Goldstein, 'Police Discretion Not to Invoke the Criminal Process: Low Visibility Decisions in the Administration of Justice', *Yale Law Journal* (1960), 69(4): 543.

[76] James Gobert and Maurice Punch, *Rethinking Corporate Crime* (Butterworths, 2003), p. 9.

prevent bribery under the Bribery Act[77]—have rendered criminal law a viable response for enforcement authorities. This is particularly so in relation to larger corporates, where the identification principle previously meant that prosecution was difficult. Thus (and irrespective on one's views of such failure offences), the question might be asked whether non-prosecution routes can continue to be justified (as responses to inadequacies in the criminal law) given that the evolving criminal law is now, arguably, equipped to target corporate crime.

Third, it has been suggested that '[c]riminal law has not so much failed as been by passed'.[78] CROs are one example of how alternative approaches were adopted as an enforcement response to corporate crime, although they have only been used by the SFO on seven occasions. CROs are still available to the SFO; however—with the advent of DPAs—they will now only be used in exceptional circumstances. In contrast, Scottish authorities are using CROs in the corporate context notwithstanding criticisms levied against the SFO when it had adopted this response. The Scottish self-reporting initiative, whereby corporates are encouraged to come forward in the hope of avoiding criminal prosecution, has been renewed annually since its inception in 2011. While there is no indication that this might change anytime soon, it is notable that an OECD 2017 evaluation expressed concern as to the use of civil settlements to resolve foreign bribery cases and recommended that Scotland should 'adopt a scheme comparable to the DPA scheme in the UK to overcome the weaknesses apparent in civil settlements, and to achieve consistency across the UK with regard to the tools available to law enforcement authorities for the resolution of foreign bribery cases'.[79]

Fourth, despite their infancy DPAs would appear to be at the heart of the enforcement response (in England and Wales) to corporate crime. The OECD evaluation considered that DPAs are

---

[77] See SFO, 'Press Release—Sweett Group PLC Sentenced and Ordered to Pay £2.25 Million After Bribery Act Conviction' (February 19, 2016); Simon Bowers, 'Construction Firm Sweett Fined Over Abu Dhabi Hotel Contract', *The Guardian* (February 19, 2016).

[78] Celia Wells, 'Corporate Crime: Opening the Eyes of the Sentry', *Legal Studies* (2010), 30(3): 370, 390.

[79] OECD, *Implementing the OECD Anti-Bribery Convention. Phase 4 Report: United Kingdom* (OECD, 2017), p. 59.

'an interesting and effective feature for sanctioning legal persons in foreign bribery cases'.[80] And it would appear that many more DPAs are in the pipeline, with suggestions that investigations into high profile corporates might be resolved by DPAs in the coming years. A significant concern that had been expressed prior to the enactment of DPAs was whether corporates could end up 'buying' their way out of the criminal justice system, however the size of fines imposed in the few cases to date has assuaged some concerns.[81] Yet, there remain concerns that the negotiation of justice results in corporates being treated differently to individuals who engage in crime. The four DPAs to date have given rise to a number of interesting points (such as the importance attached to self-report/cooperation; when a DPA will be in the interests of justice; the terms of the DPA, including financial penalties; the ability of the corporate to pay; and the discount given by the court), which will inform the development of DPA jurisprudence in the UK. More interestingly, perhaps, will be the response of the SFO when a corporate fails to abide by the terms of its DPA.

[80] Ibid.
[81] See Nicola Padfield, 'Deferred Prosecution Agreements', *Criminal Law Review* (2016): 449.

Selected Bibliography

Ainslie, Elizabeth K. 'Indicting Corporations Revisited: Lessons of the Arthur Andersen Prosecution'. *American Criminal Law Review* (2006), 43: 107.

Alge, Daniele. 'Negotiated Plea Agreements in Cases of Serious and Complex Fraud in England and Wales: A New Conceptualisation of Plea Bargaining?' *European Journal of Current Legal Issues* (2013), 19(1).

Alldridge, Peter. 'Bribery and the Changing Pattern of Criminal Prosecution'. In Jeremy Horder and Peter Alldridge (eds), *Modern Bribery Law: Comparative Perspectives* (Cambridge University Press, 2013).

Alldridge, Peter. 'Civil Recovery in England and Wales: An Appraisal'. In Colin King, Clive Walker, and Jimmy Gurulé (eds), *The Handbook of Criminal and Terrorism Financing Law* (Palgrave, 2018).

Allott, Anthony. 'The Effectiveness of Law'. *Valparaiso University Law Review* (1981), 15: 229.

Alschuler, Albert W. 'Two Ways to Think About the Punishment of Corporations'. *American Criminal Law Review* (2009), 46: 1359.

Arlen, Jennifer. 'Corporate Criminal Liability: Theory and Evidence'. In Alan Harel and Keith N. Hylton (eds), *Research Handbook on the Economics of Criminal Law* (Edward Elgar, 2012).

Arlen, Jennifer. 'Prosecuting Beyond the Rule of Law: Corporate Mandates Imposed Through Deferred Prosecution Agreements'. *Journal of Legal Analysis* (2016), 8(1): 191.

Ashworth, Andrew, and Mike Redmayne. *The Criminal Process* (5th ed, Oxford University Press, 2010).

Baker, John S., Jr. 'Reforming Corporations Through Threats of Federal Prosecution'. *Cornell Law Review* (2004), 89(2): 310.

Baldwin, John, and Michael McConville. *Negotiated Justice: Pressures to Plead Guilty* (Martin Robertson and Co Ltd, 1977).
Beale, Sara Sun. 'A Response to the Critics of Corporate Criminal Liability'. *American Criminal Law Review* (2009), 46: 1481.
Beetham, David. *The Legitimation of Power* (2nd ed, Palgrave Macmillan, 2013).
Benson, Michael L., and Sally S. Simpson. *Understanding White-Collar Crime: An Opportunity Perspective* (2nd ed, Routledge, 2015).
Bisgrove, Michael, and Mark Weekes. 'Deferred Prosecution Agreements: A Practical Consideration'. *Criminal Law Review* (2014), 6: 416.
Blumenson, Eric, and Eva Nilsen. 'Policing for Profit: The Drug War's Hidden Economic Agenda'. *University of Chicago Law Review* (1998), 65(1): 35.
Bohrer, Barry A., and Barbara L. Trencher. 'Prosecution Deferred: Exploring the Unintended Consequences and Future of Corporate Cooperation'. *American Criminal Law Review* (2007), 44: 1481.
Bottoms, Anthony, and Justice Tankebe. 'Beyond Procedural Justice: A Dialogic Approach to Legitimacy in Criminal Justice'. *Journal of Criminal Law and Criminology* (2012), 102(1): 119.
Braddock, Robert A. 'Rhetoric or Restoration? A Study into the Restorative Potential of the Conditional Cautioning Scheme'. *International Journal of Police Science and Management* (2011), 13(3): 195.
Braithwaite, John. *Crime, Shame and Reintegration* (Cambridge University Press, 1989).
Braithwaite, John, and Peter Drahos. 'Zero Tolerance, Naming and Shaming: Is There a Case for It with Crimes of the Powerful?' *Australian and New Zealand Journal of Criminology* (2002), 35(3): 269.
Bronitt, Simon. 'Regulatory Bargaining in the Shadows of Preventive Justice: Deferred Prosecution Agreements'. In Tamara Tulich, Rebecca Ananian-Welsh, Simon Bronitt, and Sarah Murray (eds), *Regulating Preventive Justice: Principle, Policy and Paradox* (Routledge, 2017).
Brooks, Allen R. 'A Corporate Catch-22: How Deferred and Non-prosecution Agreements Impede the Full Development of the Foreign Corrupt Practices Act'. *Journal of Law, Economics and Policy* (2010), 7: 155.
Campbell, Liz. 'The Recovery of "Criminal" Assets in New Zealand, Ireland and England: Fighting Organised and Serious Crime in the "Civil" Realm'. *Victoria University Wellington Law Review* (2010), 41: 15.
Carpenter, Dick M., Lisa Knepper, Angela C. Erickson, and Jennifer McDonald. *Policing for Profit: The Abuse of Civil Asset Forfeiture* (2nd ed, Institute for Justice, 2015).
Chambers, W. Bradnee. 'Towards an Improved Understanding of Legal Effectiveness of International Environmental Treaties'. *Georgetown International Environmental Law Review* (2004), 16: 501.

Cheng, Kevin Kwok-yin. 'Pressures to Plead Guilty: Factors Affecting Plea Decisions in Hong Kong's Magistrates' Courts'. *British Journal of Criminology* (2013), 53: 257.

Clarkson, C.M.V. 'Kicking Corporate Bodies and Damning Their Souls'. *Modern Law Review* (1996), 59: 557.

Clough, Edward. 'First UK Deferred Prosecution Agreement Between the SFO and a Bank'. *Allen and Overy, Litigation and Dispute Resolution Review* (April 2016).

Collins, Martin, and Colin King. 'The Disruption of Crime in Scotland Through Non-conviction Based Asset Forfeiture'. *Journal of Money Laundering Control* (2013), 16(4): 379.

Corruption Watch. 'A Failure of Nerve: The SFO's Settlement with Rolls Royce' (January 19, 2017). Available at: http://www.cw-uk.org/2017/01/19/a-failure-of-nerve-the-sfos-settlement-with-rolls-royce/ (last accessed January 28, 2018).

Cressey, Donald R. 'Negotiated Justice'. *Criminology* (1968), 5(4): 5.

Croall, Hazel. 'Combating Financial Crime: Regulatory Versus Crime Control Approaches'. *Journal of Financial Crime* (2000), 11(1): 45.

Crown Office and Procurator Fiscal Service (COPFS). *Guidance on the Approach of the Crown Office and Procurator Fiscal Service to Reporting by Businesses of Bribery Offences* (June 2017).

Crown Prosecution Service (CPS). *Adult Conditional Cautions (The Director's Guidance)* (7th ed, April 2013).

Cullen, Francis T., Gray Cavender, William J. Maakestad, and Michael L. Benson. *Corporate Crime Under Attack: The Fight to Criminalize Business Violence* (2nd ed, Routledge, 2015).

Dau-Schmidt, Kenneth G. 'An Economic Analysis of the Criminal Law as a Preference-Shaping Policy'. *Duke Law Journal* (1990): 1.

Darbyshire, Penny. 'The Mischief of Plea Bargaining and Sentencing Rewards'. *Criminal Law Review* (2000): 895.

Davis, Frederick T. 'International Double Jeopardy: U.S. Prosecutions and the Developing Law in Europe'. *American University International Law Review* (2016), 31(1): 57.

Duff, Anthony, Lindsay Farmer, Sandra Marshall, and Victor Tadros. *The Trial on Trial, Vol. 3: Towards a Normative Theory of the Criminal Trial* (Hart, 2007).

Dunford, Louise, and Ann Ridley. '"No Soul to Be Damned, No Body to Be Kicked": Responsibility, Blame and Corporate Punishment'. *International Journal of the Sociology of Law* (1996), 24: 1.

Durkheim, Emile. *The Division of Labour in Society* (The Free Press, 1997).

Fisse, Brent, and John Braithwaite. 'The Allocation of Responsibility for Corporate Crime: Individualism, Collectivism and Accountability'. *Sydney Law Review* (1988), 11: 468.

Friedrichs, David O. *Trusted Criminals: White Collar Crime in Contemporary Society* (4th ed, Wadsworth, 2009).

Gallant, Michelle. *Money Laundering and the Proceeds of Crime: Economic Crime and Civil Remedies* (Edward Elgar, 2005).

Gallie, W.B. 'Essentially Contested Concepts'. *Proceedings of the Aristotelian Society, New Series* (1956), 56: 167.

Garrett, Brandon L. 'Structural Reform Prosecution'. *Virginia Law Review* (2007), 93: 853.

Garrett, Brandon. *Too Big to Jail: How Prosecutors Compromise with Corporations* (Harvard University Press, 2014).

Gobert, James. 'Country Report: UK'. In James Gobert and Ana-Maria Pascal (eds), *European Developments in Corporate Criminal Liability* (Routledge, 2011).

Gobert, James, and Maurice Punch. *Rethinking Corporate Crime* (Butterworths, 2003).

Goldstein, Joseph. 'Police Discretion Not to Invoke the Criminal Process: Low Visibility Decisions in the Administration of Justice'. *Yale Law Journal* (1960), 69(4): 543.

Grasso, Costantino. 'Peaks and Troughs of the English Deferred Prosecution Agreement: The Lesson Learned from the DPA Between the SFO and ICBCSB Plc'. *Journal of Business Law* (2014), 5: 388.

Hampton, Philip. *Reducing Administrative Burdens: Effective Inspection and Enforcement* (March 2005).

Hasnas, John. 'The Centenary of a Mistake: One Hundred Years of Corporate Criminal Liability'. *American Criminal Law Review* (2009), 46: 1329.

Hasnas, John. 'Where Is Flex Cohen When We Need Him: Transcendental Nonsense and the Moral Responsibility of Corporations'. *Journal of Law and Policy* (2010), 19: 55.

Hendry, Jennifer, and Colin King. 'How Far Is Too Far? Theorising Non-conviction-Based Asset Forfeiture'. *International Journal of Law in Context* (2015), 11(4): 398.

Hendry, Jennifer, and Colin King. 'Expediency, Legitimacy, and the Rule of Law: A Systems Perspective on Civil/Criminal Procedural Hybrids'. *Criminal Law and Philosophy* (2017), 11(4): 733.

Henham, Ralph. 'Further Evidence on the Significance of Plea in the Crown Court'. *Howard Journal of Criminal Justice* (2002), 41(2): 151.

Henning, Peter. 'Should the Perception of Corporate Punishment Matter?' *Journal of Law and Policy* (2010), 19(1): 83.

Hensarling, Jeb (Chair). *Too Big to Jail: Inside the Obama Justice Department's Decision Not to Hold Wall Street Accountable.* Report Prepared by the Republican Staff of the Committee on Financial Services, U.S. House of Representatives (2016).
Hill, Jennifer. 'Corporate Criminal Liability in Australia: An Evolving Corporate Governance Technique?' *Journal of Business Law* (2003): 1.
Hinsch, Wilfried. 'Legitimacy and Justice: A Conceptual and Functional Clarification'. In Jorg Kühnelt (ed.), *Political Legitimization Without Morality?* (Springer, 2008).
HM Crown Prosecution Service Inspectorate (HMCPSI). *Report to the Attorney General on the Inspection of the Serious Fraud Office* (November 2012).
HM Crown Prosecution Service Inspectorate, HM Inspectorate of Court Administration, and HM Inspectorate of Constabulary. *Joint Thematic Review of Asset Recovery: Restraint and Confiscation Casework* (Criminal Justice Joint Inspection, 2010).
Home Office. *Asset Recovery Statistical Bulletin 2011/12–2016/17.* Statistical Bulletin 15/17 (September 2017).
Hough, Mike, Jonathan Jackson, and Ben Bradford. 'Legitimacy, Trust and Compliance: An Empirical Test of Procedural Justice Theory Using the European Social Survey'. In Justice Tankebe and Alison Liebling (eds), *Legitimacy and Criminal Justice: An International Exploration* (Oxford University Press, 2013).
Jefferson, Andrew. 'The Situated Production of Legitimacy: Perspectives from the Global South'. In Justice Tankebe and Alison Liebling (eds), *Legitimacy and Criminal Justice: An International Exploration* (Oxford University Press, 2013).
JUSTICE. *Negotiated Justice: A Closer Look at the Implications of Plea Bargains* (JUSTICE, 1993).
Kaiser, Gordon. 'Corruption in the Energy Sector: Criminal Fines, Civil Judgments, and Lost Arbitrations'. *Energy Law Journal* (2013), 34(1): 193.
Karstedt, Susanne. 'Creating Institutions: Linking the "Local" and the "Global" in the Travel of Crime Policies'. *Police Practice and Research* (2007), 8(2): 145.
Karstedt, Susanne. 'Trusting Authorities: Legitimacy, Trust, and Collaboration in Non-democratic Regimes'. In Justice Tankebe and Alison Liebling (eds), *Legitimacy and Criminal Justice: An International Exploration* (Oxford University Press, 2013).
Kennedy, Anthony. 'Justifying the Civil Recovery of Criminal Proceeds'. *Journal of Financial Crime* (2004), 12(1): 8.
Khanna, Vikramaditya S. 'Corporate Criminal Liability: What Purpose Does It Serve?' *Harvard Law Review* (1996), 109(7): 1477.
Khanna, Vikramaditya S. 'Corporate Crime Legislation: A Political Economy Analysis'. *Washington University Law Quarterly* (2004), 82: 95.

King, Colin. 'Using Civil Processes in Pursuit of Criminal Law Objectives: A Case Study of Non-conviction Based Asset Forfeiture'. *International Journal of Evidence and Proof* (2012), 16(4): 337.

Koehler, Mike. 'Measuring the Impact of Non-prosecution and Deferred Prosecution Agreements on Foreign Corrupt Practices Act Enforcement'. *University of California, Davis Law Review* (2015), 49: 497.

Laufer, William S. *Corporate Bodies and Guilty Minds: The Failure of Corporate Criminal Liability* (University of Chicago Press, 2006).

Lea, John. 'Hitting Criminals Where It Hurts: Organised Crime and the Erosion of Due Process'. *Cambrian Law Review* (2004), 35: 81.

Levi, Michael. 'Fraud in the Courts: Roskill in Context'. *British Journal of Criminology* (1986), 26(4): 394.

Levi, Michael. 'Legitimacy, Crimes and Compliance in "the City": *De Maximis non Curat Lex?*' In Justice Tankebe and Alison Liebling (eds), *Legitimacy and Criminal Justice: An International Exploration* (Oxford University Press, 2013).

Levi, Michael, and Nicholas Lord. 'White-Collar and Corporate Crimes'. In Alison Liebling, Shadd Maruna, and Lesley McAra (eds), *The Oxford Handbook of Criminology* (6th ed, Oxford University Press, 2017).

Lippke, Richard L. *The Ethics of Plea Bargaining* (Oxford University Press, 2011).

Lord, Nicholas. 'Establishing Enforcement Legitimacy in the Pursuit of Rule-Breaking "Global Elites": The Case of Transnational Corporate Bribery'. *Theoretical Criminology* (2016), 20(3): 376.

Lord, Nicholas. *Regulating Corporate Bribery in International Business: Anti-corruption in the UK and Germany* (Ashgate, 2014).

Lord, Nicholas, and Colin King. 'Negotiating Non-contention: Civil Recovery and Deferred Prosecution in Response to Transnational Corporate Bribery'. In Liz Campbell and Nicholas Lord (eds), *Corruption in Commercial Enterprise: Law, Theory and Practice* (Routledge, 2018).

Lord, Nicholas, and Mike Levi. 'In Pursuit of the Proceeds of Transnational Corporate Bribery: The UK Experience to Date'. In Colin King, Clive Walker, and Jimmy Gurulé (eds), *The Handbook of Criminal and Terrorism Financing Law* (Palgrave, 2018).

MacCormick, Neil. *Institutions of Law: An Essay in Legal Theory* (Oxford University Press, 2007).

Macrory, Richard B. *Regulatory Justice: Making Sanctions Effective—Final Report* (November 2006).

Markoff, Gabriel. 'Arthur Andersen and the Myth of the Corporate Death Penalty: Corporate Criminal Convictions in the Twenty-First Century'. *University of Pennsylvania Journal of Business Law* (2013), 15(3): 797.

Mazzacuva, Federico. 'Justifications and Purposes of Negotiated Justice for Corporate Offenders: Deferred and Non-prosecution Agreements in the UK and US Systems of Criminal Justice'. *Journal of Criminal Law* (2014): 249.

Miller, Andrew B. 'What Makes Companies Behave? An Analysis of Criminal and Civil Penalties Under Environmental Law' (December 2005). Available at: https://papers.ssrn.com/sol3/papers.cfm?abstract_id=471841 (last accessed January 28, 2018).

Ministry of Justice. *Consultation on a New Enforcement Tool to Deal with Economic Crime Committed by Commercial Organisations: Deferred Prosecution Agreements* (Cm 8348) (May 2012).

Ministry of Justice. *Code of Practice for Adult Conditional Cautions: Part 3 of the Criminal Justice Act 2003* (January 2013).

Ministry of Justice. *Corporate Liability for Economic Crime, Call for Evidence* (Cm 9370) (January 2017).

Moxon, David, and Carol Hedderman. 'Mode of Trial Decisions and Sentencing Differences Between Courts'. *Howard Journal of Criminal Justice* (1994), 33(2): 97.

Mulcahy, Aogán. 'The Justification of Justice—Legal Practitioners' Accounts of Negotiated Case Settlements in Magistrates' Courts'. *British Journal of Criminology* (1994), 34: 411.

Nagin, Daniel S. 'Deterrence in the Twenty-First Century'. *Crime and Justice* (2013), 42(1): 199.

Nanda, Ved P. 'Corporate Criminal Liability in the United States: Is a New Approach Warranted?' In Mark Pieth and Radha Ivory (eds), *Corporate Criminal Liability. Emergence, Convergence and Risk* (Springer, 2011).

National Evaluation of the CashBack for Communities Programme (April 2012–March 2014) Final Report (ODS Consulting, 2014).

Nicholls, Colin, Timothy Daniel, Alan Bacarese, and John Hatchard. *Corruption and Misuse of Public Office* (2nd ed, Oxford University Press, 2011).

OECD. *Phase 3 Report on Implementing the OECD Anti-bribery Convention in the United Kingdom* (March 2012).

OECD. *Implementing the OECD Anti-Bribery Convention: Phase 4 Report: United Kingdom* (OECD, 2017).

Owusu-Bempah, Abenaa. *Defendant Participation in the Criminal Process* (Routledge, 2017).

Padfield, Nicola. 'Deferred Prosecution Agreements'. *Archbold Review* (2012), 7: 4.

Padfield, Nicola. 'Deferred Prosecution Agreements'. *Criminal Law Review* (2016): 449.

Pascal, Ana-Maria. 'A Legal Person's Conscience: Philosophical Underpinnings of Corporate Criminal Liability'. In James Gobert and Ana-Maria Pascal (eds), *European Developments in Corporate Criminal Liability* (Routledge, 2011).

Pinto, Amanda, and Martin Evans. *Corporate Criminal Liability* (3rd ed, Sweet and Maxwell, 2013).

Pitt, Harvey L., and Karen L. Shapiro. 'Securities Regulation by Enforcement: A Look Ahead at the Next Decade'. *Yale Journal on Regulation* (1990), 7: 149.

Punch, Maurice. 'The Organizational Component in Corporate Crime'. In James Gobert and Ana-Maria Pascal (eds), *European Developments in Corporate Criminal Liability* (Routledge, 2011).

Raphael, Monty. *Bribery: Law and Practice* (Oxford University Press, 2016).

Ridge, Robert J., and Mackenzie A. Baird. 'The Pendulum Swings Back: Revisiting Corporate Criminality and the Rise of Deferred Prosecution Agreements'. *University of Dayton Law Review* (2008), 33(2): 197.

Lord Roskill (Chair). *Fraud Trials Committee Report* (HM Stationery Office, 1986).

Sentencing Council. *Fraud, Bribery and Money Laundering Offences: Definitive Guideline* (2014).

Sentencing Council. *Reduction in Sentence for a Guilty Plea: Definitive Guideline* (March 2017).

Serious Fraud Office (SFO). *Approach of the Serious Fraud Office to Dealing with Overseas Corruption* (July 2009).

SFO/CPS. *Deferred Prosecution Agreements Code of Practice* (2013).

Snider, Laureen, and Steven Bittle. 'The Challenge of Regulating Powerful Economic Actors'. In James Gobert and Ana-Maria Pascal (eds), *European Developments in Corporate Criminal Liability* (Routledge, 2011).

Spivack, Peter, and Sujit Raman. 'Regulating the "New Regulators": Current Trends in Deferred Prosecution Agreements'. *American Criminal Law Review* (2008), 45: 159.

Sprenger, Polly. *Deferred Prosecution Agreements: The Law and Practice of Negotiated Corporate Criminal Penalties* (Sweet and Maxwell, 2015).

Stephen, James Fitzjames. *A History of the Criminal Law of England, Vol. II* (William S. Hein Reprint: 1883).

Sutherland, Edwin H. *White Collar Crime: The Uncut Version* (Yale University Press, 1983).

Tankebe, Justice, and Alison Liebling. 'Legitimacy and Criminal Justice: An Introduction'. In Justice Tankebe and Alison Liebling (eds), *Legitimacy and Criminal Justice: An International Exploration* (Oxford University Press, 2013).

Tankebe, Justice, and Alison Liebling (eds). *Legitimacy and Criminal Justice: An International Exploration* (Oxford University Press, 2013).

Tombs, Steve, and David Whyte. *The Corporate Criminal: Why Corporations Must Be Abolished* (Routledge, 2015).

Transparency International (UK). *Deterring and Punishing Corporate Bribery: An Evaluation of UK Corporate Plea Agreements and Civil Recovery in Overseas Bribery Cases* (Transparency International, 2012).

Turk, Matthew C. 'Regulation by Settlement'. *University of Kansas Law Review* (2017), 66: 259.

Tyler, Tom R. 'Public Trust and Confidence in Legal Authorities: What Do Majority and Minority Group Members Want from the Law and Legal Authorities?' *Behavioral Sciences and the Law* (2001), 19: 215.

Tyler, Tom R. 'Psychological Perspectives on Legitimacy and Legitimation'. *Annual Review of Psychology* (2006), 57: 375.

Tyler, Tom R. 'Self-Regulatory Approaches to White-Collar Crime: The Importance of Legitimacy and Procedural Justice'. In Sally S. Simpson and David Weisburd (eds), *The Criminology of White-Collar Crime* (Springer, 2009).

Tyler, Tom R. *Why People Cooperate: The Role of Social Motivations* (Princeton University Press, 2011).

Uhlmann, David M. 'After the Spill Is Gone: The Gulf of Mexico, Environmental Crime, and the Criminal Law'. *Michigan Law Review* (2011), 109: 1413.

Uhlmann, David M. 'Deferred Prosecution and Non-prosecution Agreements and the Erosion of Corporate Criminal Liability'. *Maryland Law Review* (2013), 72(4): 1302.

US Government Accountability Office. *Corporate Crime: DOJ Has Taken Steps to Better Track Its Use of Deferred and Non-prosecution Agreements, but Should Evaluate Effectiveness.* GAO-10-110 (December 2009).

Vettori, Barbara. 'The Disposal of Confiscated Assets in the EU Member States: What Works, What Does Not Work and What Is Promising'. In Colin King, Clive Walker, and Jimmy Gurulé (eds), *The Handbook of Criminal and Terrorism Financing Law* (Palgrave, 2018).

Vogel, Mary E. 'The Social Origins of Plea Bargaining: Conflict and the Law in the Process of State Formation, 1830–1860'. *Law and Society Review* (1999), 33(1): 161.

Vogel, Mary E. *Coercion to Compromise: Plea Bargaining, the Courts, and the Making of Political Authority* (Oxford University Press, 2007).

Watson, Michael. 'The Enforcement of Environmental Law: Civil or Criminal Penalties?' *Environmental Law and Management* (2005), 17(1): 3.

Weinberger, Ota. 'Legal Validity, Acceptance of Law, Legitimacy: Some Critical Comments and Constructive Proposals'. *Ratio Juris* (1999), 12(4): 336.

Wells, Celia. *Corporations and Criminal Responsibility* (2nd ed, Oxford University Press, 2001)

Wells, Celia. 'Corporate Crime: Opening the Eyes of the Sentry'. *Legal Studies* (2010), 30(3): 370.

Wells, Celia. 'Containing Corporate Crime. Civil or Criminal Controls?' In James Gobert and Ana-Maria Pascal (eds), *European Developments in Corporate Criminal Liability* (Routledge, 2011).

Wells, Celia. 'Corporate Failure to Prevent Economic Crime—A Proposal'. *Criminal Law Review* (2017): 426.

INDEX

A
Abbott Group Ltd, 19, 34, 46. *See also* Abbot; Abbott Group
Abbot, 66
Abbott Group, 66
Abetting, 70
Ability to pay, 54, 92–94, 104, 131
Abuse, 22, 61, 112, 113
Accommodation, 2, 3, 9, 68, 118, 132–134
Accountability, 79, 109, 114, 121, 125, 127, 128, 130, 132
Accountancy, 52, 73, 83
Accounting irregularities, 22, 112
Achievable, 16
Acquittal, 12, 49
Acts, 73, 81, 123
Actus reus, 120
Admission, 8, 15, 16, 23, 24, 54, 77, 87, 93, 98, 108
Africa, 44, 84
Agent, 112
Aggravating factors, 97–98

Aiding, 70
Airbus, 6, 109
Alderman, Richard, 37, 41, 42, 48, 131. *See also* Alderman Years
Alderman Years, 38
Alexandria Library, 38
Allegations, 18, 36, 40, 54, 78, 84, 89, 110
Alternative to criminal prosecution, 45, 49
AMEC plc, 17, 39
American Bar Association, 12
Annan, Kofi, 99
Anonymity, 96
Anonymous SME, 21, 72, 83
Anti-money laundering, 78
Arthur Andersen, 73, 74
Arthur Andersen Effect, 74
Asia, 79
Asset Recovery Incentivisation Scheme (ARIS), 61, 62
Associated person, 20, 47
Attorney General's guidelines, 44

150 INDEX

Austerity, 12

B
BAE Systems, 9, 37, 119, 135
Balancing, 98
Balfour Beatty, 17, 34, 38, 39, 42
Barclays, 5, 6
Blockbuster funding, 135
Braid Group (Holdings) Ltd, 20, 48
Brand Breaks, 47
Brand-Rex Ltd, 20, 47
Brazil/Brazilian, 97, 98
Breach, 20, 47, 48, 58, 78, 80, 131
Bribery, 2, 5, 8, 16–22, 24, 35–43, 46–50, 63, 69, 76, 85–87, 90, 97, 102, 106, 109–110, 112, 133, 135, 137, 138. *See also* Bribes; Transnational bribery
Bribery Act 2010, 20–22, 45, 47, 48, 70, 76, 84–86, 90, 95, 102, 133, 137
Bribes, 21, 43, 54, 90, 91, 103
Budget, 62, 135
Budgetary constraints, 12
Burma, 78
Business community, 25, 30, 104

C
Calling to account, 9, 117, 129, 130. *See also* Calling to answer
Calling to answer, 129
answer, 73
Case investigation teams, 65
Cashback for Communities, 62, 63
Certainty, 89, 125
Certainty of punishment, 106
Chancellor of the Exchequer, 79
Charge, 2, 12, 13, 15, 127
Charge reduction, 13

Checks and balances, 114
Cheque book justice, 30
China, 97
City of London, 135
City of London police, 40
Civil action, 41, 131, 132
Civil justice, 9, 117
Civil law, 35
Civil liability, 122
Civil order, 58
Civil penalties, 125
Civil proceedings, 69, 126, 131
Civil process, 34
Civil recovery, 33–35, 41–44, 51, 56, 58, 61, 62, 64, 69, 64, 118
Civil Recovery Orders (CROs), 3, 4, 6, 7–9, 12, 14, 16, 17–20, 28, 33–36, 38–49, 53, 55, 58, 59, 63–66, 68, 71, 83, 131, 133, 134, 137
Civil Recovery Unit (CRU), 8, 16, 17, 19, 20, 34, 35, 46–48, 50, 51–53, 63
Civil sanction, 36, 58, 126
Civil settlements, 2, 3, 6, 8, 12, 36, 46, 49, 51, 52, 69, 82, 133, 137. *See also* Settlement
Code for Crown Prosecutors, 15, 43, 45, 71
Code of Practice, 85, 89
Collapsed cases, 4
Collateral damage, 5, 75, 79, 82
Collateral effects, 122
Columbia/Columbian, 78
Command and control, 37
Commercial advantage, 42
Communicative, 9, 122, 129
Companies Act 1985, 17, 38, 39, 70
Companies Act 2006, 48, 70
Compensation, 21, 58–60, 70, 75, 83, 85, 94, 113, 126, 131

INDEX 151

Compliance, 23, 25, 27, 31, 42, 59, 70, 77, 78, 83, 85, 90–92, 95, 97, 99, 101, 102, 114, 132
Compromise, 13, 78, 110, 134
Concept, 12, 14, 16, 23, 25, 28, 68
Conception, 25, 127
Conceptual framework, 11
Condemnation, 120, 127
Conditional caution, 15, 16
Confiscation, 53, 55–59, 62, 83
Conflict of interest, 57, 61, 62
Consent Order(s), 38, 39, 43, 64
Conspiracy, 21, 70, 90
Conspiracy to corrupt, 21, 22, 55, 90, 97
Consultation, 68, 69, 73, 74, 76
Controlling mind, 76, 82, 97, 120
Convention Judiciaire d'Intérêt Public (CJIP), 80
Conviction, 3, 5, 12, 15, 33, 34, 52, 62, 63, 71, 73–77, 87, 91, 99, 103, 104, 111, 118, 120, 121, 127, 130, 131, 136, 137
Cooperation, 1, 9, 24, 40, 42, 54, 59, 68, 70–72, 82, 83, 85, 86, 90, 93, 94, 102, 104, 107–109, 111, 113, 138
Coordination, 79
Corporate civil liability, 122
Corporate crime, 3–5, 7–9, 12, 14, 23, 28, 29, 34, 35, 45, 67, 68, 117, 118, 125, 126, 128, 133, 134, 136, 137
corporate financial crime, 4
Corporate criminal liability, 2, 9, 74–76, 81, 82, 118–134, 136
inadequacy, 9
Corporate culture, 78, 101
Corporate Manslaughter and Corporate Homicide Act 2007, 120
Corporate mind, 81
Corporate personality, 124
Corporate responsibility, 124
Corporate vehicle, 92
Corruption, 3–5, 8, 14, 16–19, 24, 28, 34, 36, 37, 39–44, 46, 47, 54–61, 63, 72, 75, 80, 86, 89, 96, 97, 99–103, 107–111, 118, 119, 131, 133
Corruption Watch, 101–103, 107–111
Corrupt payments, 19, 20
Costs, 2, 17–19, 21, 22, 31, 39–41, 43, 52, 53, 59, 70, 75–77, 83, 85, 90, 91, 94, 97, 98, 104, 111, 113, 126
Counselling, 70
CPS prosecutors, 67, 69
Crime and Courts Act 2013, 3, 45, 67, 69, 70, 87, 89
Crime-control, 25
Crime fighting, 5
Criminal, 9, 12, 14, 30, 36, 58, 65, 69, 98, 123, 127
non-criminal, 10
Criminal activity, 33
Criminal assets, 34
Criminal behaviour, 2, 8, 12, 23, 24, 36, 75, 82, 92, 112, 114, 121
Criminal benefit, 12, 57, 104
Criminal charges, 74
Criminal conduct, 2, 3, 36, 51, 52, 56–58, 70, 82, 95, 99
Criminal conviction, 34
Criminal enforcement, 35, 68, 77, 121, 125
Criminal Finances Act 2017, 76
Criminal intent, 81
Criminal investigation, 19, 43, 51, 53, 66, 71, 77, 97, 112
Criminalisation, 8, 23
Criminal justice, 9, 12, 23, 31
Criminal Justice Act, 57
Criminal Justice Act 1987, 4

Criminal Justice Act 2003, 13, 15, 16, 93, 130
Criminal justice system, 12–14
Criminal label, 73, 127
Criminal liability, 9, 49, 55, 76, 112, 117, 119, 121, 122, 124
Criminal law, 9, 16, 37
Criminal Law Act 1977, 21, 22, 55
Criminal outcome, 24
Criminal proceedings, 9, 16, 48, 58, 59, 129–131
Criminal process, 14, 34, 50
Criminal prosecution, 2, 3, 7–9, 18, 33, 35–38, 40, 41–45, 49, 68–70, 74, 79, 96, 102, 103, 114, 118, 119, 121, 123, 126–129, 132, 134, 136, 137
Criminal sanction, 7, 8
Criminal wrongdoing, 45, 127
Criticism, 5, 8, 39–43, 45, 50, 60, 62, 63, 65, 71, 78, 110, 134
Crown Office and Procurator Fiscal Service (COPFS), 46–51
Crown Prosecution Service (CPS), 15, 16, 50, 67, 69, 71–73, 76, 77, 85, 89, 102
Cuba, 54, 78
Culpability, 56, 85, 86, 93, 123
Culture, 77, 91, 99, 101, 102, 124, 125
Customs and Excise Management Act 1979, 70

D
Death penalty, 74
Debarment, 42, 43, 99
Deepwater Horizon, 128
Deferred Prosecution Agreements (DPAs), 3–9, 12, 14–16, 18, 21, 22, 28, 29, 34, 38, 40, 45, 47, 49, 54, 67–78, 80–98, 100–115, 118, 133, 134, 137, 138. *See also* Terms of a DPA
deferred prosecution, 9
Deficiency, 10, 30, 37, 72, 80
Delaware, 54
Democracy, 103
Department of Justice (DOJ), 54, 55, 69, 73, 74, 78, 79, 80, 88, 93, 98
DePuy International Ltd, 18, 39, 40
Detection, 84, 86, 106, 125
Deterrence, 57, 66, 74, 75, 106, 110, 114, 125, 126
Differences, 13, 73, 76
Differential enforcement, 30, 133. *See also* Differentially enforced; Differential treatment
Differentially enforced, 2, 133
Differential treatment, 30, 110, 120
Directing mind, 120
Discount, 87, 93, 104, 108, 109, 111, 138
Discretion, 75, 134, 136
Disgorgement, 18, 21, 22, 40, 42, 44, 49, 56, 70, 81, 83, 85, 88, 90, 92, 94, 97, 104–106
Disposal, 12, 62, 86
Disruption, 62
Diversion, 7, 14–16
DOJ. *See* Department of Justice (DOJ)
Donation, 70
Double jeopardy, 18, 40, 58, 69, 88
Downgrading, 9, 117
DPA Code of Practice, 69, 72, 102. *See also* Code of Practice
DPAs. *See* Deferred Prosecution Agreements (DPAs)
Drug, 1
Due diligence, 42
Due process, 13, 14, 34

INDEX 153

E
Economic, 7, 9, 24, 27, 31, 34, 61, 68–70, 73, 74, 76, 78, 79, 91, 93, 100, 103, 114, 118, 119, 121, 127, 134–136
Economic interests, 7
Effective, 14, 15, 57, 66, 68, 81, 85, 95, 106, 126, 127, 138
Egypt, 17, 38
Embargo regulations, 54
Enforcement, 2–4, 6–12, 16, 23–31, 33, 35–38, 41, 49–52, 54, 66–69, 72–78, 80–82, 88, 93, 100, 110, 114, 115, 117, 118, 120–122, 125–128, 132–134, 136, 137
Enforcement agency, 134
Enforcement authority, 25, 29, 33
Enforcement – difficulties, 7, 35, 121
England and Wales (E+W), 6, 14, 34, 36, 47, 50, 55, 61, 68, 69, 73, 76–78, 81, 82, 95, 137
Enron, 73
Enterprise Growth Market Advisors (EGMA), 21
Equality, 8, 23, 30, 82
Equal treatment, 37, 114, 120. *See also* Equality
European Union (EU), 77, 135
Evidence, 1, 3–7, 13, 15, 37, 44, 71, 74, 77, 82, 84, 91, 95, 109–111, 118, 124
Evidential difficulties, 7
Evidential stage, 71
Expert witnesses, 136

F
Failure of nerve, 102, 103, 108–111
Failure to prevent, 20–22, 47, 76, 85, 90, 97, 102, 121, 136
Fair/fairness, 7–10, 23, 25, 26, 30, 60, 72, 73, 75, 80, 87, 94, 114, 117, 133, 134

False accounting, 22, 97, 98, 112
Family business, 120
Federal Reserve, 79
F.H. Bertling group, 3
F.H. Bertling Ltd, 118
Fictional entity, 122
Financial Conduct Authority (FCA), 50, 113
Financial orders, 21, 83, 90, 92, 110
Financial penalty, 21, 22, 64, 70, 83, 85, 87, 88, 90–94, 97, 104
Financial reporting obligations, 70
Financial Services and Markets Act 2000, 70
Financial Services Authority (FSA), 79, 80
Fine/fines, 5, 6, 31, 47, 53, 54, 56–59, 62, 77, 78, 87, 105, 106, 112, 130, 131, 137, 138
Ford Pinto, 126
Foreign Corrupt Practices Act (FCPA), 42, 48, 74, 93, 132
Foreign Exchange (Forex), 80
Forensic accountants, 50, 53
Forgery and Counterfeiting Act 1981, 70
France, 80
Fraud, 2, 4–6, 14, 22, 36–39, 45, 47, 64–66, 81, 83, 87, 93, 96, 106, 112, 113, 135, 136
Fraud Act 2006, 22, 70, 112
Front-running, 81
Full Code Test, 15, 71
Funding, 63, 135

G
Global corporate elites, 24
Global elites, 31
Global resolution, 18, 40
Global settlements, 35, 53, 54, 59
Gray, Nigel, 48
Greece/Greek, 39

Green, David, 4, 5, 38, 43, 44, 47, 77, 82, 84, 94, 106, 134, 135. *See also* Green Years
Green Years, 42
Gross profit, 20, 21, 44, 47, 48, 90, 92–94, 104, 105. *See also* Profits
Guidelines on Plea Discussions in Cases of Serious or Complex Fraud, 14
Guilty admission, 8, 23
Guilty plea, 7, 13, 59, 79, 87, 93. *See also* Guilty admission

H
Hampton, Philip, 127. *See also* Hampton report
Hampton report, 127
Hensarling, Jeb, 79
Hensarling report, 80. *See also* Hensarling, Jeb
HM Crown Prosecution ServiceInspectorate (HMCPSI), 45, 61, 64–66
Home Office, 61
HSBC, 78–81
Hybrid, 38, 67

I
Identification principle, 8, 68, 81, 120, 121
Ideological, 7–9, 37, 68, 81, 114, 118, 134
Impact, 74, 82, 91, 93, 99, 102, 103, 106, 120, 134
Implementation, 8, 53, 67–70, 83, 90, 91, 97, 114
Inadequacy, 9, 118, 134
Incentives, 13, 108, 109
Incentivisation, 7, 11, 35, 61, 62, 90, 98, 100, 104. *See also* Incentives
Independence, 135

India, 97
Indictment, 71, 78, 85, 90
Individually liable, 114
Indonesia, 54, 55, 58–61, 97
Inducement, 7, 11, 43
Innospec, 35, 36, 53–62, 65
Insolvent/insolvency, 92–94
Interests of justice, 68, 75, 90, 92, 93, 97, 100, 101, 109, 138
Interference, 9, 37, 119
Intermediary/Intermediaries, 18, 39, 90, 98
Internal compliance/training programme, 70, 114
Internal control mechanisms, 42
Internal investigation, 72, 86, 90, 91
International Tubular Services Ltd (ITS), 20, 46, 66
Investors, 31, 41, 42, 77, 132
Iran, 78
Iraq, 54–56, 58, 60, 61
Irregular payments, 17, 39
ITS. *See* International Tubular Services Ltd (ITS)

J
Johnson and Johnson, 39
Jones Day, 84
Judges, 12, 64, 114
Judicial approval, 70
Judicial oversight, 54, 71, 75, 76
Judicial supervision, 5. *See also* Judicial oversight
Judiciary, 31, 35, 54, 55, 110. *See also* Judges
Justice, 2, 4, 7–16, 23, 25–27, 29–31, 36, 45, 54, 56–59, 61, 63, 64, 69, 72–74, 76, 79–82, 84, 88, 106, 108, 112, 114, 117, 118, 120, 121, 125–127, 130, 132–134, 136
Juvenile/Juvenile offenders, 14

INDEX 155

K
Kazakhstan, 46

L
Labelling, 64, 73
Lack of certainty, 88
Left idealism, 134
Legal persons, 123
Legitimacy, 3, 7, 8, 10, 14, 16, 23–29, 31, 34–37, 63, 68, 75–77, 82, 109, 114, 121, 133–135. *See also* Legitimate
 deligitimation, 31
 illegitimate, 29
 legality, 28, 29, 35
 legitimacy deficit, 30, 72, 80
 legitimation, 29, 31, 114
 normative validity, 28, 30
Legitimate, 8, 9, 12, 16, 23–28, 31, 35, 47, 63, 82, 89, 115, 117, 118, 120, 130, 135
Leniency, 1
Leveson, Brian, 70, 84, 86, 87, 90, 91, 93–95, 97–104, 107–112
Libya, 78
Light touch, 80
Loss, 4, 42, 99, 102, 135

M
Mabey and Johnson, 18, 40
Mabey Engineering (Holdings) Ltd, 18, 41, 131
MacAskill, Kenny, 63
MacMillan Publishers Ltd, 18, 40
Macrory, Richard B., 127. *See also* Macrory Report
Macrory Report, 127
Malaysia, 97
Market abuse, 113
Market position, 39
Mens rea, 123

Mexico/Mexican, 78
Ministério Público Federal, 97, 98
Ministry of Justice, 7, 15, 16, 68, 69, 73, 74, 76, 118
Money laundering, 34, 62, 78–81, 87, 136. *See also* Anti-money laundering
Money Laundering Regulations 2017, 70
Monitoring, 24, 59, 71, 77
Moral, 7, 8, 23, 26, 28, 114, 120, 122, 124
Motivation, 45, 75, 76
Multiplier, 93
MW Kellogg Ltd, 17, 39

N
National Crime Agency (NCA), 50, 135, 136
National Economic Crime Centre (NECC), 135
Nation states, 23, 24
Negotiated justice, 3, 7, 8, 11–14, 16, 23, 28–31, 37, 134, 138
Negotiated outcomes, 88
Negotiated resolution, 40
Negotiated settlement, 102, 119, 132
Negotiation, 3, 6–9, 11–14, 16, 23, 24, 28–31, 35, 37, 38, 40, 43, 45, 49, 50, 53, 64, 65, 67–73, 75, 76, 82, 84, 86–89, 96, 100, 102, 104, 106, 108, 112–115, 118, 119, 132–134, 138
 negotiated non-contention, 3
 negotiating justice, 8, 11
 preference, 3
Negotiation of justice, 12, 29, 138
New normal, 2
NGOs, 29, 31
Nigeria, 97
Non-contention, 4, 35, 75, 96, 133
 contention, 9

Non-criminal measures, 2, 36. *See also* Non-criminal responses
Non-criminal responses, 2, 36
Non-criminal sanction, 8, 23
Non-penal consequences, 103
Non-prosecution agreements (NPAs), 69, 74, 76
Normative, 7–9, 23, 24, 26–29, 68, 75, 77, 115, 118, 127, 129, 130, 134
Northern Ireland, 16

O
Objective, 26, 29, 36
Obstructing justice, 73
OECD. *See* Organisation for Economic Co-operation and Development (OECD)
OECD Anti-Bribery Convention, 88, 114
OECD Convention on Combatting Bribery of Foreign Public Officials in International Business Transactions 1997, 24. *See also* OECD Anti-Bribery Convention
OECD Phase 3 evaluation, 65
OECD Phase 4 evaluation, 66
Offender, 15, 55, 56, 110, 130
Office of Foreign Asset Control (OFAC), 54, 55
Oil for Food Programme, 54
Omissions, 81, 123
Open justice, 56
Openness, 8, 95
OPL. *See* Oxford Publishing Ltd (OPL)
Organisation for Economic Co-operation and Development (OECD), 6, 24, 34, 36, 37, 45, 49, 50, 63–66, 69, 70, 88, 106, 108, 109, 114, 137

Osborne, George, 79
Overseas, 19, 31, 37, 43, 44, 46, 79
Oxford Publishing Ltd (OPL), 6, 19, 38, 42–44, 63, 65
Oxford University Press (OUP), 43, 44
Oxford University Press East Africa (OUPEA), 43, 44
Oxford University Press Tanzania (OUPT), 43, 44

P
Para-criminal concept, 68
Parent company, 17, 39–41, 90, 91, 94, 95
Par value, 48
Payment irregularities, 17, 38
Penalty, 49, 55, 58–60, 74, 81, 87, 89, 95, 104, 108, 130
Perception, 7, 8
Performance, 10, 28, 30, 36, 37, 75, 81, 110
Personality, 124, 125
Persuasive, 81, 114
Plea, 13, 14, 55, 56, 59, 64
Plea agreement, 59, 64
Plea-bargaining, 12, 13, 136. *See also* Plea
POCA. *See* Proceeds of Crime Act (POCA)
Policing for profit, 61, 62
Policy, 8, 9, 15, 31, 36, 37, 67–69, 72, 76, 82, 95, 104, 106, 109, 122, 127, 133, 135
Policy transfer, 82
Political dimension, 135
Pragmatic, 7–9, 37, 68, 94
Precedent, 75, 76, 108
Preference, 3, 35, 36, 62, 133
Preferential treatment, 93, 89
Pre-trial diversion, 14

INDEX 157

Prevention, 47, 77, 126
Preventive, 15, 69, 72
PricewaterhouseCoopers LLP, 85
Primary response, 7, 134
Procedural fairness, 114
Procedural justice, 23, 25–27, 114, 120
Procedural protections, 34
Proceeds of Crime, 3, 61
Proceeds of Crime Act 2002 (POCA), 3, 33, 63, 70
Procuring, 70
Profits, 17, 21, 22, 39, 42, 49, 56, 57, 70, 83, 90, 101, 106, 112, 113
Proportionate, 15, 16, 57, 66, 72, 75, 87, 94, 114
Proprietary action, 33
Prosecution rhetoric, 96
Prosecutor, 4, 5, 12, 15, 31, 43, 45, 57, 60, 62, 63, 67–73, 75–78, 87, 89, 96, 98, 118, 134, 135
Proximity, 120
Public, 7, 30, 45, 56, 96
Public discourse, 114
Public interest, 5, 7, 36, 52, 56–58, 71, 72, 80, 84, 85, 92, 100–104, 109–111, 128, 135
Publicly, 35, 96, 113
Public oversight, 111
Public policy, 104
Public wrong, 129
Punishment, 9, 49, 78, 106, 118, 121, 122, 127, 129–131, 134
Punitive, 14, 74, 75, 131

Q
Quality, 74, 75

R
Recidivism, 126
Reform, 37, 73, 75, 77, 114, 126

Reformation, 9, 68
Regulated community/regulated communities, 7, 10, 26, 72, 73, 115, 125
Regulation, 7, 11, 25, 114, 132, 133
Rehabilitation, 15
Relationship, 40, 118, 136
Reparation, 16, 75
Reputation, 42, 49, 128
Resolution, 18, 40, 43, 47, 62, 65, 69, 74–76, 85, 88, 102, 133, 137
Resources, 9, 12, 44, 49, 100, 125, 133, 134
Resourcing, 104, 106, 135
Responsibility, 87, 114, 119, 121, 122, 124, 125, 127–129
Restitution, 81, 125
Rhetoric, 6, 16, 38, 96, 111
Risk, 12, 49, 52, 65, 72, 79, 81, 91, 94, 102, 106, 108
Rolls Royce, 4, 72, 83, 86, 87, 92, 96, 98, 99, 101, 103, 104, 106, 108–110, 114, 115, 135
Rolls Royce plc, 22, 97, 102–104, 107–111
Roskill Report, 4
Rule of law, 10, 35, 75, 78, 82, 103
Russia, 97
Rwanda, 40

S
Sanction, 8–10, 23, 35, 36, 58, 66, 76, 78, 82, 117, 125, 126, 128, 132, 134, 138
Sapin II Law (France), 80
Saudi Arabia, 135
Scotland/Scottish, 6, 8, 16, 34, 35, 38, 45–50, 62, 63, 66, 69, 137
Scottish authorities, 6
Scrutiny, 64, 78, 110, 126
SEC. *See* Securities and Exchange Commission (SEC)

Securities and Exchange Commission
  (SEC), 54, 55, 69, 73, 78, 89
Secondary consequence, 122
Self investigation, 82, 86
Self-report, 2, 5, 6, 17–22, 35, 36,
  38, 39, 44, 46–53, 72, 84, 86,
  87, 90, 91, 93–95, 98, 100, 104,
  106–109, 111, 137, 138
Sentence, 1, 13, 15, 36, 54–56, 59,
  87, 93, 102–104, 108, 122, 130,
  131
Sentence discount, 104. *See also*
  Discount
Sentencing Council Guidelines, 87
Serious and Organised Crime Unit
  (SOCU), 49–51, 53
Serious Fraud Office (SFO), 2–6, 8,
  16–19, 21, 22, 26, 34–50, 53–55,
  57, 59–69, 72, 77, 82, 84, 85,
  90, 94, 96, 97, 100, 103, 104,
  106–115, 118, 119, 131, 132
  collapsed cases, 4
  data loss, 4
  failed investigations, 4, 134–138
  reprieve, 5
  threats of being abolished, 4, 5
Seriousness, 16, 44, 51, 85, 90, 91,
  102, 129, 134
Settlement, 2–6, 8, 12, 14, 28,
  35–37, 41, 43, 44, 46, 48–55,
  59, 62, 64, 65, 77, 97, 102–104,
  108–111, 119, 133
Severity, 75, 76, 106
SFO Proceeds of Crime Unit, 61
SFO. *See* Serious Fraud Office (SFO)
Share dividends, 17, 18, 39, 41, 131
Shared values, 77, 129
Shareholders, 17, 41, 77, 82, 95, 102,
  103, 122, 130–132
Share price, 77
Shares, 48, 113. *See also* Share price
Small and Medium Enterprises
  (SMEs), 82, 90, 92, 96

Smith and Ouzman, 118
Social equality, 7, 134
Societal condemnation, 9, 74, 75,
  121, 125, 127, 128. *See also*
  Condemnation
Socio-economic development, 103
South Africa, 80
Southwark Crown Court, 70, 84–90,
  92–94, 97, 102–104, 107–111,
  114
Stability, 79
Stanbic Bank Tanzania, 21, 84, 85
Standard Bank, 21, 65, 70, 72, 83–89,
  92, 93, 107, 115
Statement of facts, 73, 77, 78, 113
Stigma/Stigmatic, 15, 73, 77, 130
Stolen Asset Recovery Initiative
  (StAR), 39–41, 131
Strict liability, 76
Structured irresponsibility, 125
Subsidiary, 17–19, 38–41, 43, 44, 46,
  54, 66, 92, 95, 112, 119, 132
Success, 12, 73, 81, 82, 131
Sudan, 78
Suspended, 71, 85, 90
Sutherland, Edwin, 2

T
Tanzania, 21, 43, 84, 88
Tax evasion, 76, 80
Tax reduction, 85, 90, 97
Terms of a DPA, 70, 77, 82, 113
  fair, reasonable and proportionate,
    72, 75, 87, 94
  repayment term, 110
Tesco Plc, 5, 22, 83, 92, 112–114,
  120
Tesco Stores Limited, 22, 112, 113
Thailand, 97
Theft Act 1968, 22, 70, 112
Third parties, 17
Time period, 71

Too big to jail, 15, 78
Tipping point, 108
Transnational, 4
Transnational bribery, 6, 45, 83
Transnational corporate bribery, 24
Transparency, 3, 8, 35, 42–45, 49, 56, 63–66, 75, 80, 135
  lack, 3
  transparently, 7
Transparency International, 45
Transparent, 56
Treasury, 135
Trial, 4, 12–14, 49, 112, 113, 127, 129, 130, 132
Two-stage test, 71

U
Uganda, 40
UK. *See* United Kingdom
Unaoil, 6, 109
UNESCO, 17
United Kingdom (UK), 4, 8, 13, 18, 34, 37, 39, 43, 54, 55, 58, 60, 68, 69, 75, 76, 78–82, 84, 87, 88, 90, 98, 99, 102, 106, 110, 112, 114, 118, 124, 131–135, 137, 138
United Nations (UN), 24, 54, 99
United Nations Convention Against Corruption 2003 (UNCAC), 24
United States (US), 9, 12–15, 18, 21, 22, 40, 54–59, 56, 69, 73–82, 85, 88, 90, 93, 97, 98, 106, 108, 109

Unlawful activity, 20, 47
UN sanctions, 18
US Treasury, 80
US. *See* United States (US)

V
Value Added Tax Act 1994, 70
Vicarious liability, 81

W
Wardle, Robert, 37
Whistleblower, 72, 107
White-collar, 136
White-collar crime, 2, 3, 23, 28, 30, 133, 136
White collar criminals, 30
Willing participant, 17, 39
World Bank, 18, 40, 43, 44

X
XYZ, 90–96, 108
XYZ Ltd, 65, 72, 87, 90, 92–94, 107, 108, 114. *See also* Anonymous SME; XYZ

Z
Zambia, 40